"Most school data attest what has happened and what students can and cannot do, and thus looks backward. COVID-19-era teaching has amplified the value of seeking evidence to also look forward. Data needs to help us make decisions about the next best teaching and learning steps and be bold yet confident in making predictions of future learning. Stepan Mekhitarian invites us to be bold, look forward, learn from our experiences during COVID-19, harness technology, and accelerate learning."

"'Formative assessment' is not about assessment. Instead, it is a teaching philosophy that uses evidence (from tests, student work, student voice about their progress, and teacher observation) to optimally make judgments about the next best teaching and learning steps. This message is evident in every chapter of these two complementary books—for teachers and leaders—which makes Dr. Mekhitarian's message so powerful. Worthwhile data must lead to actions, acceleration, advancing confidence, and advising about impact for leaders, teachers, and students."

—**John Hattie,** Emeritus Laureate Professor in the Graduate School of Education at the University of Melbourne

"Timely, relevant, and immediately applicable, these companion books by Dr. Mekhitarian offer just-in-time, responsive strategies for both teachers and school leaders interested in using formative assessment data to support students' learning in today's rapidly changing education landscape."

—**Kasia Faughn,** Assessment Communication Program Manager, Sacramento County Office of Education

"Dr. Stepan Mekhitarian provides a timely resource for public schools to reimagine their student-data practices. These companion books succinctly address the climate in which we are

educating and how to improve instruction despite recent gaps in performance data. Leveraging the speed and accuracy of technology to transform formative assessment practices is how we, as educators, accelerate learning and dig ourselves out of learning loss caused by the pandemic."
—**Robyn Anders,** Coordinator of Instructional Technology, Burbank Unified School District

"Dr. Mekhitarian is a sought-after subject matter expert in the state of California who shares his vast knowledge of the formative assessment process in a way that is both robust and easy for readers to understand. These fantastic companion books include space to reflect on thought-provoking prompts that help us engage in the learning in a deeper and more meaningful way, and the tips called out throughout the books are pure gold!"
—**Nikki Antonovich,** Coordinator, Center for Student Assessment and Program Accountability, Sacramento County Office of Education

"Dr. Mekhitarian is a seasoned educational leader who tirelessly continues his firm commitment to instructional innovations and academic excellence. His companion books are essential for any educator interested in using formative data to make great decisions for students. They are practical, informative, effective, inspiring, and timely, especially as we come out of the pandemic and reflect on what's next in education. The companion books are undoubtedly must-have resources for professional development in schools, districts, and teacher preparation programs."
—**Silva S. Karayan,** Professor Emeritus of Education, California Lutheran University

"Stepan's innovative approach on formative assessment in a virtual setting has had a vast impact on our academy. The way he dives deep into the purpose and importance of meaningful

checks for understanding has changed the way our teachers create, implement, and analyze assessments."
—**Erika Tumminelli,** Principal, Salinas City Virtual Academy

"Dr. Mekhitarian's two new companion books make the cogent case that formative assessments are not just checks for understanding, but key tools in fostering systemic and organizational change for the benefit of all students. By following the suggested activities, teachers and administrators can begin to dialogue about the role of formative assessments with respect to their schools' mission and vision, and figure out how to maximize the impact of these tools given a changing educational landscape spurred on by the pandemic and recent technological advances."
—**Paul Hsu,** Director and Co-Founder, Lotus Creek Foundation and t space Taiwan

"Dr. Mekhitarian provides a comprehensive, step-by-step process to help teachers and school leaders make formative data the primary driver in decision-making. His books offer key insights as to how schools can build a sense of shared accountability and urgency to meet the needs of all students. As a school district leader, Dr. Mekhitarian knows firsthand the challenges of building a strong data culture. His recommendations are practical and actionable, featuring timely advice on leveraging technology and empowering teachers and administrators to use formative data to promote equity in schools."
—**Evan Bartelheim,** Project Director, Accountability & Data Literacy, Los Angeles County Office of Education

"As an educational leader, we are asked all the time, 'How do you know students are learning?' Formative assessments give real-time insight into student learning and progress.

Dr. Mekhitarian gives his readers practical and actionable advice so that school and district leaders can confidently answer that question, 'We know because . . .' I highly recommend this book to anyone seeking effective, research-based strategies that focus on accelerating student learning. Anyone can pick it up, apply the strategies, and make a real, measurable difference for students!"
—**Kelly King,** Assistant Superintendent,
Glendale Unified School District

"The principle that grounds my work is that all students deserve to thrive in an inclusive environment supported by adults who put them at the center of every conversation. Dr. Mekhitarian's innovative approach to post-pandemic formative assessment provides an actionable plan to guide school/student/teaching improvement efforts."
—**Vivian Ekchian,** Superintendent,
Glendale Unified School District

"This book is a must-read for all school leaders and educators. It contains valuable, ready-to-use resources to lead school teams in utilizing real-time-data regularly and systematically to measure progress and develop concrete action plans.
—**Juanita Shahijanian,** Principal,
John Marshall Elementary School

"Dr. Mekhitarian is an expert in formative assessment. This book represents an important resource for schools and districts wanting to use data to inform instruction and professional development."
—**Joshua Einhorn,** Grants Officer, Michael D. Eisner College of Education,
California State University Northridge

"Dr. Mekhitarian's companion books are texts that provide educators with the tools they need in order to outline how to best utilize data. These texts allow readers to carve out their paths towards data analysis and establish best practices for utilizing the data to support learning. I have worked with Dr. Mekhitarian on many occasions to create systems to best incorporate the ideas suggested in his books. We have been successful in our results and continue to further develop and incorporate his strategies. I highly recommend these texts."

—**Mary Mardirosian,** Assistant Principal, Herbert Hoover High School

"These books are a staple that need to be in the hands of every instructional leader and classroom teacher. Dr. Stepan Mekhitarian provides valuable insight on how to effectively utilize formative data to improve student learning. Moreover, he addresses how to foster a data-driven culture, providing actionable steps that will help every school site reach its full potential."

—**Natalie Kontogiannis,** Director of Curriculum, Instruction, and Innovation, AGBU Manoogian-Demirdjian School

"The development of technology has delivered more data to schools than ever before. In these two companion volumes, Dr. Mekhitarian lays out a roadmap for teachers and administrators to leverage the data schools collect into timely actions for both the larger organization and the classroom. This work provides the connection between the data-rich world of high-stakes school evaluation and the inside-the-classroom moves made by each teacher. Using side-by-side texts focused on simple moves for the teacher and school leader with supportive and practical implementation tips, Dr. Mekhitarian's work will allow your school to develop a vision around what educators can learn from the use of formative data and how it will positively impact schools, teachers, and students."

—**Elias Miles,** Assistant Superintendent, Fillmore Unified School District

"In a time when many educators are struggling to address the current challenges, Stepan brings his expertise and authenticity to provide support in this space. These two companion books provide practical steps to infuse formative assessment with educational technology to foster a growth mindset and increase student learning. Stepan effectively communicates both a vision and practical steps to operationalize this vision. These books are accessible for teachers and organizational leaders with a focus on increasing student agency and success."

—**Dave Chun,** Director, Mathematics,
Sacramento County Office of Education

"A companion text to Mekhitarian's book focused on real-time data collection for teachers, this text supports instructional leaders as they seek to improve almost any aspect of their school at the organizational level. Schools often collect a plethora of data but do not always use it for data-based decision-making, or they wait until the end of the year to review and analyze data. This innovative text provides myriad strategies for how to collect meaningful real-time data and, more importantly, how teams can collaborate to analyze and use that data proactively for school improvement around equity, social justice, and educational success. Using a Plan-Do-Study-Act cycle, in conjunction with the tables, tech tips, worksheets, and interactive planning guides offered by the author, school leaders can make decisions that are responsive, timely, and based on immediate data collection and analysis."

—**Wendy W. Murawski, PhD,** Eisner Endowed Chair & Executive Director, Center for Teaching & Learning, California State University Northridge

"Dr. Mekhitarian pushes our thinking to consider the many data points available to schools and districts as they consider how to make data-informed decisions regularly to support all students and promote equity. He challenges us to move beyond the annual summative data frenzy and leverage new and existing technology to establish systems that provide real-time supports for students and families."

—**Jessica Conkle,** Director l, Los Angeles County Office of Education

"These two books provide school leaders and teachers with a wealth of knowledge and practical applications for implementing formative assessment practices and using data in real time to inform both classroom instruction and professional learning. These books are particularly timely in the context of the transition back to classroom-based instruction from time spent in distance or hybrid learning experiences. Educators are immersed in a changing landscape brought on not only by pandemic-based impacts on learning contexts but also by challenging academic standards and ever-evolving real-world contexts into which our students will become future workers and citizens. These books can support educational leaders and classroom educators to select high-quality assessment strategies, collect immediately actionable data to feed back into teaching and learning, and apply both the assessment practices and the data to promote social justice and ensure equity and access to rigorous learning and academic outcomes."

—**Sally J. Bennett-Schmidt,** Retired Director of Assessment, San Diego County Office of Education

Harnessing Formative Data for K-12 Leaders

Harnessing Formative Data for K-12 Leaders prepares school and district leaders to re-evaluate how real-time formative data can inform policy, planning, and professional development. The importance of effective formative data use has escalated since the expansion of distance learning and the integration of digital education tools, which have impacted the consistency, accuracy, availability, and actionability of data points that leaders rely on. This book's strategic insights into actionable, organizational-level formative data use will yield differentiated supports for schools to foster greater academic outcomes, a culture of equity and social-emotional well-being, and students' readiness for college, career, and lifelong learning. Each chapter includes connections to social justice, best practices for applying data points and field-tested tips for technology integration, and a host of interactive planning guides to support implementation.

Stepan Mekhitarian is Director of Innovation, Instruction, Assessment & Accountability at Glendale Unified School District, California.

Also Available from Routledge Eye On Education
(www.routledge.com/k-12)

Artificial Intelligence in Schools
A Guide for Teachers, Administrators, and Technology Leaders
Varun Arora

Leading Schools Through Trauma
A Data-Driven Approach to Helping Children Heal
Michael S. Gaskell

Abolitionist Leadership in Schools
Undoing Systemic Injustice Through Communally Conscious Education
Robert S. Harvey

The Influential School Leader
Inspiring Teachers, Students, and Families Through Social and Organizational Psychology
Craig Murphy and John D'Auria

Making Technology Work in Schools
How PK-12 Educators Can Foster Digital-Age Learning
Timothy D. Green, Loretta C. Donovan, Jody Peerless Green

Integrating Computer Science Across the Core
Strategies for K-12 Districts
Tom Liam Lynch, Gerald Ardito, Pam Amendola

Harnessing Formative Data for K-12 Leaders

Real-time Approaches to School Improvement

Stepan Mekhitarian

NEW YORK AND LONDON

Cover image: Shutterstock

First published 2023
by Routledge
605 Third Avenue, New York, NY 10158

and by Routledge
4 Park Square, Milton Park, Abingdon, Oxon, OX14 4RN

*Routledge is an imprint of the Taylor & Francis Group,
an informa business*

© 2023 Stepan Mekhitarian

The right of Stepan Mekhitarian to be identified as author of this work has been asserted in accordance with sections 77 and 78 of the Copyright, Designs and Patents Act 1988.

All rights reserved. No part of this book may be reprinted or reproduced or utilised in any form or by any electronic, mechanical, or other means, now known or hereafter invented, including photocopying and recording, or in any information storage or retrieval system, without permission in writing from the publishers.

Trademark notice: Product or corporate names may be trademarks or registered trademarks, and are used only for identification and explanation without intent to infringe.

Library of Congress Cataloging-in-Publication Data
Names: Mekhitarian, Stepan, author.
Title: Harnessing formative data for K-12 leaders : real-time approaches to school improvement / Stepan Mekhitarian.
Description: New York, NY : Routledge, 2023. | Includes bibliographical references and index. | Identifiers: LCCN 2022019930 (print) | LCCN 2022019931 (ebook) | ISBN 9781032154831 (hardback) | ISBN 9781032156682 (paperback) | ISBN 9781003245247 (ebook)
Subjects: LCSH: Computer managed instruction. | School improvement programs—Data processing.
Classification: LCC LB1028.46 .M45 2023 (print) | LCC LB1028.46 (ebook) | DDC 371.33/4—dc23/eng/20220706
LC record available at https://lccn.loc.gov/2022019930
LC ebook record available at https://lccn.loc.gov/2022019931

ISBN: 978-1-032-15483-1 (hbk)
ISBN: 978-1-032-15668-2 (pbk)
ISBN: 978-1-003-24524-7 (ebk)

DOI: 10.4324/9781003245247

Typeset in Palatino
by Apex CoVantage, LLC

Contents

Foreword xvii
Preface xix
Acknowledgments xxiii
About the Author xxv

PART I
**The Need to Reevaluate How We Use Data
in Our Organizations** 1

Introduction 3
  ♦ Advancements in Technology Changing
    Formative Data Use 5
    ♦ Instructional Technology Creates New
      Opportunities to Gather and Use Data 6
    ♦ Identifying *Actionable* Data From a Sea
      of Data Points 8
  ♦ Loss of Consistent Summative Data From
    Previous Academic Years 10
    ♦ Continuity of Data Points Disrupted by
      Changing Metrics 11
    ♦ Continuity of Data Points Disrupted by
      Changing Events 12
  ♦ Concerns About Data Reliability Due to
    Limited Measures 12
  ♦ Key Takeaways 13

1 Your Organization's Vision and Beliefs 15
  ♦ Assessing Your Organization's Vision 17
  ♦ Reflecting on Your Beliefs About Student
    Learning and Your Role 21

- ♦ Where Formative Data Fits In 24
- ♦ Key Takeaways 26

2 **The Impact of Formative Data on Student Success** 29
- ♦ Formative Data Fosters Educators' Growth Mindset 31
- ♦ Formative Data Informs Planning and Focus Areas 37
- ♦ Formative Data Facilitates Differentiation and Promotes Equity 39
- ♦ Key Takeaways 42

PART II
Effective Formative Data Use for Leaders 43

3 **Effective Formative Data Use to Drive Organizational Change**.............................45
- ♦ How *Actionable* Is the Data You Are Gathering?........47
- ♦ How *Timely* Is the Data You Are Gathering?...........53
  - ♦ How Soon Will You Be Able to Act On the Data?..56
- ♦ How Much Data Do You Need? 56
- ♦ How Much Time Will It Take to Collect the Data, and Will You Be Able to Address All the Data You Collect? 57
- ♦ Key Takeaways 60

4 **Using Instructional Technology to Effectively Address Formative Data**..............................61
- ♦ Efficiently Gathering Formative Data 63
  - ♦ Systematize as Much as Possible 64
  - ♦ Make the Data Easy to Access.......................67

- Identifying and Addressing Validation Concerns to Ensure Broader Impact................70
- Implementing a Collaborative Plan-Do-Study-Act Cycle to Address Data..........................72
- Key Takeaways 77

5 **Analyzing Formative Data Collaboratively to Identify and Celebrate Best Practices**................79
- PLCs Using the PDSA Cycle 82
- Peer Observations—In-Person and Virtual............87
- Professional Development Linked to Formative Data Page 91
- Including a Wide Variety of Departments to Maximize Perspective and Expertise.................94
- Key Takeaways 95

6 **Building a Data-Driven Culture of Innovation** 97
- Re-envisioning Professional Development on Formative Data for All Educators....................99
- Reflecting on the Focus on Summative and Formative Data 105
- Fostering a Data-Driven Organizational Culture 112
  - Success Celebration Events With Best Practice Sharing.................................115
- Key Takeaways 118

Conclusion 121

References 125
Index 129

Foreword

We have entered arguably the most critical turning point in education in our recent history—a turning point that could propel us forward to this generation's learning model or one that we could overlook as we tinker at the edges with transformation. We have already seen and experienced the possibilities of the power of formative data in the classroom, but have we opened the gates to leverage formative data for transformation and organizational innovation?

Dr. Stepan Mekhitarian has written a critical book at this intersection in which we find ourselves as leaders of a system that has struggled to innovate. This book is a roadmap for how we can situate ourselves with discipline, strategy, and consistency at the helm of innovation. The leader's role is not only to develop a collaborative vision, but also to establish the culture and set the course to achieve the vision. This is accomplished through a dogged commitment to creating within your school or district environment, the conditions for teachers, staff, and students to remain in a constant space of growth and innovation. Formative data is key to charting the course.

Formative data is a tool that we, as leaders, can use to make effective decisions and adjustments to our plans. It is precisely what we ask teachers to use every day to help determine the strategies they will employ with individual students, and it is how we coach them to make adjustments in their classrooms, especially when students are not making the desired progress and learning gains. Formative data practices are literally at the heart of innovation.

At our company LINC, we view the teachers who consistently leverage formative data practices as generative practitioners, or "pedagogical problem solvers." We view leaders who leverage formative data practices as the models for how to create innovative cultures within their schools.

In this book, Stepan provides practical guidance for how to draw on formative assessments. He starts by reevaluating our current lens and then provides structures for how leaders can effectively use data in their organizations for a variety of purposes: implementing technology, collaborating toward best practices, sustaining cultures of innovation, and more. Enjoy this book and dive into an exciting approach to transformative, data-driven leadership.

Jason Green and Tiffany Wycoff,
Co-authors of *Blended Learning in Action*

Preface

The changing educational landscape brought about by the transition to distance learning means leaders must rethink how to generate and use formative data to inform planning. This book is designed to prepare organizational leaders to reevaluate how they use formative data to inform policy, planning, and professional development. After analyzing the benefits of formative data to student success, we will explore current challenges, such as limited actionable data points from prior years, concerns about data reliability during distance learning, and a saturation of data points created from the increased use of technology. We will then review how technology can be harnessed to address these challenges by prioritizing timely, actionable formative data; collaboratively analyzing the data and identifying best practices; and building capacity through data-driven self-monitoring. Using actionable formative data to drive planning, policy, interventions, and instruction will lead targeted and differentiated supports for schools that will ultimately lead to greater student outcomes and equity to ensure all students succeed and become lifelong learners. The flowchart presented on the next page highlights the journey through the book, including how each chapter informs the subsequent one to create a clear path from vision to implementation.

The guide is designed as a companion to *Harnessing Formative Data for K-12 Teachers*, which focuses on formative data to inform instructional practice. These books are timely as schools and districts across the country prepare to transition back to on-campus learning and face a new reality regarding formative data. Effective use of formative data has always been a quality of high-performing educators, but its importance has been heightened since the transition to distance learning, which has impacted the consistency, accuracy, availability, and actionability of data points teachers and leaders rely on to make decisions to support student learning and equity. With limited past data points and increased proficiency and experience with instructional technology during distance learning, educators must reevaluate their philosophies on formative data points, how they generate them, and how they apply them to their practice.

Both books focus on effectively using formative data in the technology-driven, post–distance learning educational landscape with the ultimate goal of enhancing student learning and fostering equity. The companion book targets formative data in the classroom to inform instruction, while this book discusses formative data on an organizational level with topics ranging from attendance to college preparedness. They highlight connections to each other and emphasize strategies and best practices that apply to both, including opportunities to show how classroom formative data can inform organizational planning.

This book includes:

- Implementation Tips on using technology to gather formative data, differentiating support using technology, implementing a Plan-Do-Study-Act (PDSA) cycle to continually gather and assess formative data, and collaboratively identifying and sharing best practices to maximize impact.
- Worksheets and tables to guide readers through the various steps of identifying and analyzing actionable formative data.
- Interactive planning guides to navigate the Plan-Do-Study-Act cycle.
- Tech Tips to address logistical challenges and maximize actionable data analysis.
- Formative Data for Social Justice features to ensure equity and access.
- Connections to organizational formative data companion book.

Part I: The Need to Reevaluate How We Use Data in Our Organizations

Changing Data Considerations Due to . . . *(Introduction)*
♦ Advancements in Technology Changing Formative Data Use
♦ Loss of Consistent Summative Data From Previous Academic Years
♦ Concerns About Data Reliability Due to Limited Measures

Your Organization's Vision and Beliefs *(Chapter 1)*
♦ Assessing Your Organization's Vision
♦ Reflecting on Your Beliefs About Student Learning and Your Role
♦ Where Formative Data Fits In

The Impact of Formative Data on Student Success *(Chapter 2)*
♦ Formative Data Fosters Educators' Growth Mindset
♦ Formative Data Informs Planning and Focus Areas
♦ Formative Data Facilitates Differentiation and Promotes Equity

Part II: Effective Formative Data Use for Leaders

Effective Formative Data Use to Drive Organizational Change *(Chapter 3)*	Using Instructional Technology to Effectively Address Formative Data *(Chapter 4)*	Analyzing Formative Data Collaboratively to Identify and Celebrate Best Practices *(Chapter 5)*
♦ How *Actionable* Is the Data You Are Gathering? ♦ How *Timely* Is the Data You Are Gathering? ♦ How Much Data Do You Need? ♦ How Much Time Will It Take to Collect the Data, and Will You Be Able to Address All the Data You Collect	♦ Efficiently Gathering Formative Data ♦ Identifying and Addressing Validation Concerns to Ensure Broader Impact ♦ Implementing a Collaborative Plan-Do-Study-Act Cycle to Address Data	♦ PLCs using the PDSA cycle ♦ Peer Observations—In-Person and Virtual ♦ Professional Development Linked to Formative Data Page ♦ Including a Wide Variety of Departments to Maximize Perspective and Expertise

Building a Data-Driven Culture of Innovation *(Chapter 6)*
♦ Re-envisioning Professional Development on Formative Data for All Educators
♦ Reflecting on the Focus on Summative and Formative Data
♦ Fostering a Data-Driven Organizational Culture

Acknowledgments

I am eternally grateful to the people in my life who consistently supported and inspired me to give back to others. Writing this book would be impossible without the care and dedication of my parents, Vahe and Gretta, who instilled in me a love for learning from an early age. As immigrants fleeing a war-torn country, they emphasized that education in the United States would be the path to pursue my dreams, and I work every day to make that concept a reality for all students. I also want to thank my wife, Lara, whose steadfast encouragement and love helped me bring this book to life. I am also grateful to colleagues throughout my career in education who believed in me, challenged me to innovate and pursue opportunities to have a greater impact on student learning, and set an example for prioritizing students' success and well-being at all times. Their inspiration drives me to constantly push for new ways to advance student learning.

About the Author

Dr. Stepan Mekhitarian serves as the Director of Innovation, Instruction, Assessment, and Accountability for Glendale Unified School District, and he was one of the main leaders responsible for transitioning the large district to distance learning in response to the COVID-19 pandemic. Stepan previously served as the Coordinator of Data and Blended Learning in Los Angeles Unified School District. He has been passionate about instructional technology and data-driven decision making since his first year as a public school teacher. He has a wide breadth of experience in classroom and leadership positions and holds degrees from the University of California at Los Angeles, Harvard, and Loyola Marymount University (LMU). Stepan's doctoral research at LMU's Educational Leadership for Social Justice Program focused on the skills and training needed to effectively implement blended learning across schools and systems. He is a Google Certified Trainer, a Microsoft Innovative Educator, Blended Learning Universe Expert Advisor, and served as lecturer for the Instructional Technology for School Leaders course at LMU. In his spare time, he enjoys travel and spending time with his family and dog, Luna.

Part I
The Need to Reevaluate How We Use Data in Our Organizations

Introduction

Part I: The Need to Reevaluate How We Use Data in Our Organizations

Changing Data Considerations Due to . . . *(Introduction)*
♦ Advancements in Technology Changing Formative Data Use
♦ Loss of Consistent Summative Data From Previous Academic Years
♦ Concerns About Data Reliability Due to Limited Measures

NECESSITATE NEED TO REVISIT VISION

Your Organization's Vision and Beliefs *(Chapter 1)*
♦ Assessing Your Organization's Vision
♦ Reflecting on Your Beliefs About Student Learning and Your Role
♦ Where Formative Data Fits In

WHICH GUIDE FORMATIVE DATA ROLE AND ITS IMPACT

The Impact of Formative Data on Student Success *(Chapter 2)*
♦ Formative Data Fosters Educators' Growth Mindset
♦ Formative Data Informs Planning and Focus Areas
♦ Formative Data Facilitates Differentiation and Promotes Equity

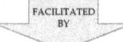
FACILITATED BY

Part II: Effective Formative Data Use for Leaders

Effective Formative Data Use to Drive Organizational Change *(Chapter 3)*	Using Instructional Technology to Effectively Address Formative Data *(Chapter 4)*	Analyzing Formative Data Collaboratively to Identify and Celebrate Best Practices *(Chapter 5)*
♦ How *Actionable* Is the Data You Are Gathering? ♦ How *Timely* Is the Data You Are Gathering? ♦ How Much Data Do You Need? ♦ How Much Time Will It Take to Collect the Data, and Will You Be Able to Address All the Data You Collect?	♦ Efficiently Gathering Formative Data ♦ Identifying and Addressing Validation Concerns to Ensure Broader Impact ♦ Implementing a Collaborative Plan-Do-Study-Act Cycle to Address Data	♦ PLCs using the PDSA cycle ♦ Peer Observations—In-Person and Virtual ♦ Professional Development Linked to Formative Data Page ♦ Including a Wide Variety of Departments to Maximize Perspective and Expertise

WHICH WILL LEAD TO

Building a Data-Driven Culture of Innovation *(Chapter 6)*
♦ Re-envisioning Professional Development on Formative Data for All Educators
♦ Reflecting on the Focus on Summative and Formative Data
♦ Fostering a Data-Driven Organizational Culture

Advancements in Technology Changing Formative Data Use

We are undoubtedly living in a rapidly evolving period of technological advancement that is changing how we do things. How we deposit checks, order food, and access directions all look different than they did from not so long ago, and they will probably continue to change in the coming years. In addition to the on-demand and immediate-access nature of these advancements, one characteristic is common among most new innovations: the availability of real-time information. We no longer look at static maps or weather predictions based on previous years; we expect to see real-time traffic patterns and weather predictions based on live satellite data. This real-time data expectation has not migrated wholesale to education yet as many educators continue to rely on summative data points that are weeks or months old to inform planning and instruction. This is partly due to the traditional assessment approaches employed in schools for decades. However, with the influx of technology in recent years and the technological expertise developed during the distance learning experience, the stage is set to take advantage of tech tools to use a real-time data approach to inform planning.

••

Actionable formative data accessibility and use can accelerate learning and shorten response times for reaching students who need additional support.

••

This is particularly crucial in post-pandemic leadership teams as the phrase "learning loss" takes hold across the country. Concerns about lost learning during distance learning fill conversations, even though the evidence for such loss has yet to be validated. In any case, the best way to address any perceived loss is through learning acceleration, which in turn can only happen by maximizing instructional efforts by utilizing real-time data. Actionable formative data accessibility and use can accelerate learning and shorten response times for reaching students who need additional support. In this book, we will explore how organizations can develop a robust formative data system that provides timely access to inform decisions and accelerate programs to rapidly impact student success. We'll start with the technology that is available to facilitate the development of the formative data system.

Instructional Technology Creates New Opportunities to Gather and Use Data

There is a growing focus on effective organizational data use through the use of technology. Piety (2019) states, "[Data-driven decision making] literature shows a significant and growing body of work studying organizational capacity for using data. Organizational capacity includes belief systems, cultural factors, and professional development" (p. 396). The technology for easily accessing real-time formative data points is available, but it alone will not create the opportunities for actionable next steps. A different vision is necessary, one that creates a sense of urgency around student achievement, prioritizes personalized responses to the data points to ensure all students succeed, and encourages innovative thinking to address challenges that have persisted for years. Without this vision, the benefits of formative data on student learning will remain limited. Luckin et al. (2017) explain,

> whilst technology has done much to support the more routinised aspects of recordkeeping, monitoring and assessment, and has begun to offer capacity for data-sharing between teachers, parents, learners and other stakeholders, this capacity and the richer, more formative aspects of students' technology-enhanced learning (TEL) data have remained difficult to operationalise, capture and evaluate. (p. 87)

This can change with the exponential increase in technology access in recent years, particularly due to the distance learning experience.

••

Real-time formative data on these topics can dramatically increase the impact and timeliness of your organization's efforts to support students, but clear systems will need to be developed to make data access clear, easy, and actionable.

••

Establishing an organizational focus on innovation is critical because it encourages looking at formative data differently and fosters conversations around the new possibilities for serving students. Luckin et al. (2017) adds,

> Schools should see themselves as innovation networks (Hargreaves, 2008). In order for this to happen, teachers need to be encouraged and supported in their engagement in a systematic inquiry into their own practices, thus enabling schools to capture and benefit from the emergent innovations that arise in and through the everyday practice of teachers as they respond to specific issues arising in the local context. (p. 95)

These practices ultimately lead to the development of new systems to support student learning with timely data to identify areas of focus and checks on progress. Formative data points can lead to effective instruction in the classroom, as researchers Shirley and Irving (2014) explain: "By promoting the use of interactive student tasks and providing both teachers and students with rapid and accurate data on student learning, [instructional technology] can provide teachers with necessary evidence for making instructional decisions about subsequent lessons" (p. 56). They can also inform organizational plans to address a wide variety of student needs, including attendance, mental health and wellness, safety, and graduation support. Real-time formative data on these topics can dramatically increase the impact and timeliness of your organization's efforts to support students, but clear systems will need to be developed to make data access clear, easy, and actionable. Data points housed in several locations without a coherent connection will complicate accessing the needed information, ultimately stifling efforts and limiting impact.

TECH TIP

Formative data is often gathered from a variety of sources, including your student information system, standards-based interim assessments, and surveys. As much as possible, try to use one universally accessible platform to gather and organize all the data points, even if they are pulled from multiple sources. An intranet website that is protected and includes links to the different data sources is one option. Having the data points in one place can help identify patterns and connections to facilitate effective planning. It can also help users organize the data in different ways to uncover patterns and trends that can inform next steps.

Identifying *Actionable* Data From a Sea of Data Points

As you begin developing the foundations of your formative data system, it won't take very long to realize that in our current data-rich age, it is very easy to become overwhelmed by the number of data points available to use and the seemingly countless ways we can house and present them. Data points can be filtered by multiple demographic factors and can include a wide variety of topics: how do we decide which ones to prioritize as we consider how we will build our formative data system?

I regularly face this question in my role as the Director of Innovation, Instruction, Assessment & Accountability at Glendale Unified School District. I am responsible for developing systems to make data analysis clear and impactful and often receive requests for data points from school sites and other departments. I can provide massive data files with enough information to keep school teams busy analyzing for hours, but I encourage teams to reconsider analyzing data points that may not be actionable. To navigate the countless data points available and provide the most critical ones, I ask one question: how will these data points impact planning and instruction to impact student achievement? Our students—especially those who are at-risk—need real-time supports and cannot wait for weeks of analysis before we can identify next steps. Any data point schools use must be timely and actionable, but what does that look like? How do you know which data points are actionable?

If you begin with the data points provided and try to determine how to make them actionable, you will find success from time to time. Instead of the data points driving your next steps, consider what you want to do and which data points are required for you to proceed. That ensures that your data analysis efforts are designed from the outset to be actionable because they are developed around the action plan. In my role as data lead, I start by asking what school sites are hoping to accomplish to determine which data points they will need to get the program off the ground or to track progress. Keep the end in mind as you consider which data points you will prioritize as you develop your actionable formative data plan.

••

If you begin with the data points provided and try to determine how to make them actionable, you will find success from time to time. Instead of the data points driving your next steps, consider what you want to do and which data points are required for you to proceed.

••

> **FORMATIVE DATA FOR SOCIAL JUSTICE**
>
> To close the achievement gap, formative data must provide actionable next steps to ensure all students get the support needed to succeed. As you consider data points to include in your analysis, consider how they will inform next steps. If connections to actionable next steps cannot be made, consider other data points instead. Consistently reinforce to the team that this work must directly connect to student success.

Loss of Consistent Summative Data From Previous Academic Years

Another consideration is the absence of summative data that occurred as a result of the COVID-19 pandemic. Many statewide assessments and accountability measures were waived during the pandemic years, resulting in limited summative data points to inform planning in the following year. In our district, we used to utilize these summative data points during summer planning sessions to identify patterns and trends around areas of strength and focus for the upcoming year. From these starting points, formative data points would be collected throughout the year to assess progress. Without these summative data points, schools had to place heavier emphasis on formative data points, including prioritizing their use early in the school year. This circumstance increased formative data use over summative data—a welcome shift as formative data points are far more actionable and therefore more directly impactful on student achievement. Even as summative data points return and accountability measures are reinstated, the importance of formative data use is now clear to many schools and will hopefully continue to take precedence over less timely summative data to inform planning and instruction.

CONNECTION TO COMPANION BOOK

Data points from the prior year may not be readily available or reliable, as was the case during the pandemic. In the absence of prior year data points, there was a heightened focus on formative data from the current year both in the classroom and at the organizational level. The companion book stresses the importance of using current year formative data daily to inform instruction and planning, while this book focuses on using formative data regularly to inform the work of leadership teams.

Continuity of Data Points Disrupted by Changing Metrics

Yet another consideration is the inconsistency in data point collection between years, adding to the limited impact on student achievement by summative data points. Often, summative data points vary from year to year based on new regulations or decisions on what to report and how to report the data, making it difficult to track progress over time or determine the effectiveness of implemented action plans. Formative data points do not present this challenge as they are generated in real-time and utilized right away, suggesting that even if metrics change, you can still get the data you need to inform planning and directly impact learning.

TECH TIP

As you consider your organization's plan for formative data gathering and analysis, be sure to design it from the beginning as "future-proof" so it is minimally impacted by changing conditions. For example, when we developed our formative data dashboard modeled after the California School Dashboard, we included a feature that would adjust our dashboard if the state dashboard shifted the cutoffs for various performance levels. This step keeps the system current and allows users to focus instead on actionable next steps.

Continuity of Data Points Disrupted by Changing Events

Also, consider how data points can be disrupted by changing events. The COVID-19 pandemic is arguably the most prevalent example of how circumstances outside the district can impact the data points we have access to and use, but there are many other events that could affect the consistency of the data over multiple academic years. Changes in political leadership, state and federal assessment regulations, and advances in technology are just a few examples of factors that can impact the data points we collect and their consistent availability. If you look at the current accountability and assessment systems in place in your state, you can almost certainly trace them back to only a few years ago as change is the only constant. These changes are yet another reason to prioritize formative data points, which are always timely and never out-of-date.

Concerns About Data Reliability Due to Limited Measures

Finally, inconsistent and sometimes limited access to summative data points can lead to a lack of trust in the reliability of the data. For example, the summative assessments in California during the COVID-19 pandemic were shortened and administered remotely, leading several educators to wonder aloud about their use relative to other years. Data points are only as useful as the trust educators put in them, so establishing their reliability is critical. With formative assessments, there are few data points each time and they are recently gathered, leading to increased reliability and applicability. This need for consistency and reliability pushes us to reevaluate how we look at data and how we can develop innovative approaches to data analysis that increase the impact on student success. Advancements in technology can improve reliability and the timeliness of data points, but it is ultimately the organization's vision that will drive how formative data is used.

●●●

If you look at the current accountability and assessment systems in place in your state, you can almost certainly trace them back to only a few years ago as change is the only constant. These changes are yet another reason to prioritize formative data points, which are always timely and never out-of-date.

●●●

Key Takeaways

In this chapter, we explored the need to reevaluate how we approach data analysis based on advancements in technology, the loss of consistent summative data from previous academic years, and concerns about data reliability due to limited measures. All of these factors drive us to find more impactful ways to utilize data, particularly in real-time to maximize student achievement. Updates to our approach cannot be made, however, until we establish a clear organizational vision for data analysis based on our beliefs and commitments. The next chapter will help us look critically at the vision that will drive our work.

1

Your Organization's Vision and Beliefs

Part I: The Need to Reevaluate How We Use Data in Our Organizations

Changing Data Considerations Due to ... (Introduction)
- Advancements in Technology Changing Formative Data Use
- Loss of Consistent Summative Data From Previous Academic Years
- Concerns About Data Reliability Due to Limited Measures

NECESSITATE NEED TO REVISIT VISION

Your Organization's Vision and Beliefs (Chapter 1)
- Assessing Your Organization's Vision
- Reflecting on Your Beliefs About Student Learning and Your Role
- Where Formative Data Fits In

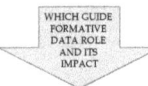
WHICH GUIDE FORMATIVE DATA ROLE AND ITS IMPACT

The Impact of Formative Data on Student Success (Chapter 2)
- Formative Data Fosters Educators' Growth Mindset
- Formative Data Informs Planning and Focus Areas
- Formative Data Facilitates Differentiation and Promotes Equity

FACILITATED BY

Part II: Effective Formative Data Use for Leaders

Effective Formative Data Use to Drive Organizational Change (Chapter 3)	Using Instructional Technology to Effectively Address Formative Data (Chapter 4)	Analyzing Formative Data Collaboratively to Identify and Celebrate Best Practices (Chapter 5)
◆ How *Actionable* Is the Data You Are Gathering? ◆ How *Timely* Is the Data You Are Gathering? ◆ How Much Data Do You Need? ◆ How Much Time Will It Take to Collect the Data, and Will You Be Able to Address All the Data You Collect?	◆ Efficiently Gathering Formative Data ◆ Identifying and Addressing Validation Concerns to Ensure Broader Impact ◆ Implementing a Collaborative Plan-Do-Study-Act Cycle to Address Data	◆ PLCs using the PDSA cycle ◆ Peer Observations—In-Person and Virtual ◆ Professional Development Linked to Formative Data Page ◆ Including a Wide Variety of Departments to Maximize Perspective and Expertise

WHICH WILL LEAD TO

Building a Data-Driven Culture of Innovation (Chapter 6)
- Re-envisioning Professional Development on Formative Data for All Educators
- Reflecting on the Focus on Summative and Formative Data
- Fostering a Data-Driven Organizational Culture

Assessing Your Organization's Vision

This new educational environment requires a rethink of how we view our goals as educators and the vision necessary to achieve them. But as we all know, change—especially organizational change—can be difficult to implement. Researcher John Hattie (2009) explains,

> The key issue is less how to change, but why we do not. In a fascinating study, Shermer (1997) researched why we tend (often passionately) to believe in ideas even when they do not work. He attributed this to an over reliance on anecdotes, dressing up one's beliefs in the trappings of science or pedagogical language and jargon, making bold claims, relying on one's past experiences rather than others' experiences, claiming that one's own experience is sufficient evidence, and circular reasoning (I am doing it so it must be ok) . . . New and revolutionary ideas in teaching will tend to be "resisted rather than welcomed with open arms, because every successful teacher has a vested intellectual, social and even financial interest in maintaining the status quo. If every revolutionary new idea were welcomed with open arms, utter chaos would be the result" (Cohen, 1985, p. 35). We have an uphill task. (p. 252)

Indeed, change—especially one steeped in innovation—does not come easy at the organizational level. Furthermore, making a change that moves from practice driven by anecdotes as described to one driven by regularly gathered and assessed data is a significant departure from many organizations' comfort zones. Making updates to an organizational vision is not a task to be taken lightly, and many organizations revisit their vision only when dramatic events or market patterns force the change.

A shift in vision implies a rethink to how the organization moves forward, leading to concerns about whether it will stray too far from its original intent. Look at automobile manufacturers who have begun to scramble to shift their vision from internal combustion engines to electric propulsion. Some have new taglines and new logos for the first time in decades, while others have presented their new vision for what transportation will look like. A vision rethink is more than new marketing materials, however. It will ultimately impact what products the company produces, where it spends its resources, and what it expects the long-term impacts of its efforts to be. It drives decisions and creates a destination for all stakeholders to envision and work toward. As educators who are preparing students for a future world we do not fully understand, we must be ready and eager to adapt and reevaluate our vision as needed to ensure our students' success.

••

A shift in vision implies a rethink to how the organization moves forward, leading to concerns about whether it will stray too far from its original intent.

••

The notion of continuous progress and self-assessment must be synonymous with educational leadership. Anderson et al. (2010) states, "When schools aspire to continuous progress there is an expectation that they, too, will make use of such data to better pinpoint problems, assess their current status, and learn their way forward" (p. 293). While updating the vision often can lead to confusion and disillusionment about the organization's direction, designing a vision that includes language acknowledging a consistent strive for improvement using data can ensure that it remains timely and reinforces an organization-wide growth mindset. Researcher Dweck (2007) explains, the cardinal rule of the growth mindset is: Learn! And like the fixed mindset, the growth mindset comes with three more rules that help students reach their goal: . . . 1: Take on challenges . . . 2: Work hard . . . 3: Confront your deficiencies and correct them.   (p. 6)

To start, reflect on your current organizational vision and what role data-driven decision-making plays in it. Consider when it was last reevaluated, how it informs policies and initiatives, and how successful the organization has been in implementation over the years. With your team, use Figure 1.1 to reflect on your current vision. We will refer back to your vision in this chapter as we determine how prioritizing formative data can fit in.

FIGURE 1.1 Your Current Organizational Vision

What is your current organizational vision?	How often is it reevaluated? When was the last time?	What role does data play in determining its implementation and updates?

CONNECTION TO COMPANION BOOK

The companion book explores the vision each teacher establishes in the classroom to promote growth mindset, equity, and a desire to become lifelong learners through the use of formative data. These visions should be connected in substance to the organizational vision that promotes the same goals. If classrooms and boardrooms are sharing the same message about the vision for student learning, one will enhance the other and lead to greater success.

Review the language of your current organizational vision and look for words that indicate a commitment to *all* students' success. A strong vision that prioritizes social justice is designed to serve the needs of all students regardless of their learning disabilities, language proficiency, socioeconomic background, or other demographics. This can only be accomplished if learning is differentiated to meet students' needs, and differentiation can only be effective if it is data-driven. If real-time formative data is used, differentiation will be more timely and more precise, leading to greater effectiveness. Therefore, we can conclude that including real-time, formative data in our vision will lead to greater differentiation, which in turn will lead to greater success for all students in your organization. Whether your organizational vision focuses on the success of all students through a differentiated model depends on your team's beliefs about student learning and what role you believe you should play in shaping the vision.

••

Including real-time, formative data in our vision will lead to greater differentiation, which in turn will lead to greater success for all students in your organization.

••

••

FORMATIVE DATA FOR SOCIAL JUSTICE

Your organizational vision must undoubtedly reflect a strong emphasis on social justice, regardless of its demographic makeup. Every educational organization is composed of a diverse group of learners with unique learning modalities, interests, and challenges. Ensuring the success of all students must be a core tenet of your organizational vision, and it should be clearly displayed, referenced, and promoted at all times. Including language in your vision that emphasizes the goal of serving all students using differentiation reinforces your focus on social justice for the entire community.

••

Reflecting on Your Beliefs About Student Learning and Your Role

To lead with data-driven decisions, we must be comfortable with data analysis ourselves. Reviewing data is typically not part of an organizational vision because it is sometimes viewed as a granular or arduous process that is out of place in a high-level statement about our goals, but this omission also sets expectations about how we approach our decision-making process. Without data-driven reflections on progress, we are simply hoping that our actions are getting us closer to our vision, and hope alone is not a strategy. Sun et al. (2016) explains,

> Even though school leaders realize that helping teachers learn data use is their responsibility, this is not being implemented in some schools. This is partly due to the fact that most principals themselves do not have training on how to use data to inform either instruction or their school leadership. That said, our research did reveal some effective practices principals can enact to help teachers use data. Principals' modeling data use, developing and visually presenting to teachers various spreadsheets and diagrams of student data analysis results, attending principal PD themselves, having individual conferences and providing individual support, and providing on-going multiple differentiated PD opportunities for teachers could enhance teachers' commitment to engage themselves in data use and to alter their teaching practices to enhance the learning of each student. (p. 28)

Indeed, leaders must emphasize the importance of using data to differentiate for all students, and while data analysis does not need to be mentioned verbatim in the vision, a clear focus on informed differentiation should drive the effort to meet the needs of all students.

> Without data-driven reflections on progress, we are simply hoping that our actions are getting us closer to our vision, and hope alone is not a strategy.

A vision driven by a commitment to differentiate to meet the needs of all students sends a message to the entire organization that we must view our progress regularly and make updates to our plans as needed to ensure student success. This commitment extends to everyone in the organization, including:

- Teachers using real-time, formative data to inform instruction and planning.
- Student services departments using real-time formative data to develop plans to address attendance and behavioral trends.
- Financial services departments using formative data in conjunction with other departments to determine if the prioritized expenditures are maximizing student achievement.
- Student health and wellness departments using formative data to determine the impact of the organization's efforts to positively influence students' physical and mental well-being.

Of course, collaboration within the organization will significantly improve these outcomes. For example, teachers can provide valuable insight on attendance trends and students' socioemotional well-being, while the technical department can speak to the benefits of affordable devices that can serve students' needs. By looking at formative data points together and collaboratively determining next steps, more cohesive and comprehensive action steps will result to serve students. Creating an organizational culture that regularly focuses on practice and outcomes at all levels takes time and buy-in and requires thoughtful reflection on our roles as educators and our beliefs about student achievement. First, there must be widespread belief that all students can succeed and that each team member will do whatever it takes to improve student learning and growth. Second, each team member must know what success looks like in their particular area and how to measure it. If these two elements are embedded throughout the organization, the stage is set for creating a vision that offers differentiated supports and programs to meet the needs of all students. Take a moment to reflect on the current status of your organization using Figure 1.2. What do

FIGURE 1.2 Current Organizational Beliefs and Formative Data Use

What beliefs about student achievement are prevalent in your organization?	
Which departments are using formative data regularly to inform next steps?	
How do you know?	
What systems are in place to guide this process?	
How does your organizational vision support these ideas?	

IMPLEMENTATION TIP

Any organizational vision requires buy-in from members in order to impact their plans and actions. Consider how you will engage members of your organization in reflecting on their beliefs about students' learning and where formative data fits into that belief. Members must consider their personal philosophies on formative assessment use, multiple and varied opportunities to demonstrate mastery, data review processes, and more. Have frank conversations with your team about their beliefs regarding formative data as part of the organizational vision. You will most likely not reach complete agreement, but the conversation can reveal priorities, interests, and beliefs to help generate greater buy-in over time.

you know about the beliefs on student achievement throughout the departments and schools? Which departments and schools utilize formative data regularly? How is formative data used to inform differentiation to meet the needs of all students?

Where Formative Data Fits In

To make formative data use a central part of your organization's vision, you will need to develop systems for regular analysis of real-time data, reflection, and action plan implementation across the organization. The data will need to be presented in a format that is easy to understand and encourages connection to conclusions. Nyland (2018) explains, "The most effective [data] systems collect as much student performance data as possible, parse through the data using advanced analysis techniques, and then present patterns and trends back to the instructor or teacher using visual techniques" (p. 523). This is a lot of work required to determine data-driven next steps, and it will become increasingly difficult to complete these steps on a regular basis unless systems are established to simplify the process and keep the focus on next steps.

When I first started leading data analysis sessions at school sites, I quickly noticed that the majority of our time was used on accessing the data points and understanding what they meant; in an hour-long session, as much as 40 minutes would sometimes be devoted to accessing the data and making sense of it, leaving only a few minutes to actually plan next steps. Developing a system to facilitate the sessions dramatically shifted this trend. I developed an online document that included step-by-step directions for accessing the data as well as screenshots and short screencasts all hyperlinked to help simplify finding the data points in focus. Whenever possible, direct links to the data points were included. Questions and prompts were also added in a table to guide the discussion on what the data points meant and what questions they raised. From there, prompts and activities guided participants through the conversation and design of next steps to address the findings. Everything needed for the data analysis process—access directions, links to the data points, guiding questions, and links to resources to address the findings—was included in an organized document to shift the focus to next steps. Before long (and after developing comfort with the document over a few sessions), we were spending the overwhelming majority of our time on data analysis and planning actionable next steps.

As you develop your new organizational vision that focuses on personalized supports based on formative data, be sure to plan out the details so that data analysis becomes a regular part of your culture. Making time for real-time data analysis can become exceedingly difficult once the school year is underway and urgent matters pop up, especially on broad topics such as the vision of the organization and where it is headed. Meeting frequently to assess high-level progress toward making the vision a reality may not be the most effective use of time, but neglecting to reflect on your vision can be detrimental as well. Find the right balance, and plan ahead to ensure your vision becomes a reality. With your leadership team, discuss the following:

- When will you meet to assess progress toward your vision?
- How will you use formative data to inform next steps?
- How often will you meet and why?
- What system will you use to easily track data?

Also, consider how you will share this vision with your board and get buy-in to ensure goal alignment. Board members undoubtedly have tremendous influence over the direction of the organization, and if they do not see the value of formative data to drive planning and supports, your efforts will yield limited results. Plan how you will share this vision with them and how you will explain the benefits of formative data, particularly if their backgrounds are in fields outside education. Give this step as much time as needed so the work can accelerate once everyone is aligned; as the saying goes, "move slow so you can move fast." Add the specifics for your plan in Figure 1.3.

FIGURE 1.3 New Organizational Vision and Logistical Planning

What is your new organizational vision?	
How will you share the vision with your board and get their buy-in?	
When will you meet to assess progress toward your vision?	
How will you use real-time formative data to inform next steps?	
How often will you meet and why?	
What system will you use to easily track data?	

CONNECTION TO COMPANION BOOK

Just like formative assessment data in the classroom, formative data at the organizational level must be actionable. In the classroom, formative data informs instruction, while at the organizational level, formative data informs policy and initiatives. In both cases, the data points inform next steps. Next steps may be slower to implement at the organizational level compared to a classroom, but in both cases, use real-time data as much as possible.

Key Takeaways

In this chapter, we explored your current organizational vision and how applicable it is to the students in your schools. We reflected on your organizational beliefs about student learning and your role as an educator in bringing your vision to life. Finally, we developed a revised vision that put real-time formative data front and center to ensure that the vision meets the needs of all students. Shifting the culture of an organization will take more than a new vision; it will require shifts in how educators view their roles, their beliefs, and their commitment to all—not most—students. This change will take time and a strong understanding of formative data and where it fits into the vision. In the next chapter, we will understand how formative data fosters educators' growth mindset, informs planning and focus areas, facilitates differentiation, and promotes equity. We will then be ready to develop the systems to make the vision a true driver for the organization.

TECH TIP

When collaboratively developing your organizational vision, emphasize that technology is a catalyst for learning, not the goal. Technology does not need to be referenced in the vision itself, even if it will be utilized to develop a formative data gathering and analysis system. The vision must prioritize ensuring the learning and success of all students.

2

The Impact of Formative Data on Student Success

Part I: The Need to Reevaluate How We Use Data in Our Organizations

Changing Data Considerations Due to ... (Introduction)
- Advancements in Technology Changing Formative Data Use
- Loss of Consistent Summative Data From Previous Academic Years
- Concerns About Data Reliability Due to Limited Measures

NECESSITATE NEED TO REVISIT VISION

Your Organization's Vision and Beliefs (Chapter 1)
- Assessing Your Organization's Vision
- Reflecting on Your Beliefs About Student Learning and Your Role
- Where Formative Data Fits In

WHICH GUIDE FORMATIVE DATA ROLE AND ITS IMPACT

The Impact of Formative Data on Student Success (Chapter 2)
- Formative Data Fosters Educators' Growth Mindset
- Formative Data Informs Planning and Focus Areas
- Formative Data Facilitates Differentiation and Promotes Equity

FACILITATED BY

Part II: Effective Formative Data Use for Leaders

Effective Formative Data Use to Drive Organizational Change (Chapter 3)	Using Instructional Technology to Effectively Address Formative Data (Chapter 4)	Analyzing Formative Data Collaboratively to Identify and Celebrate Best Practices (Chapter 5)
♦ How *Actionable* Is the Data You Are Gathering? ♦ How *Timely* Is the Data You Are Gathering? ♦ How Much Data Do You Need? ♦ How Much Time Will It Take to Collect the Data, and Will You Be Able to Address All the Data You Collect?	♦ Efficiently Gathering Formative Data ♦ Identifying and Addressing Validation Concerns to Ensure Broader Impact ♦ Implementing a Collaborative Plan-Do-Study-Act Cycle to Address Data	♦ PLCs using the PDSA cycle ♦ Peer Observations—In-Person and Virtual ♦ Professional Development Linked to Formative Data Page ♦ Including a Wide Variety of Departments to Maximize Perspective and Expertise

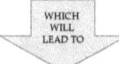
WHICH WILL LEAD TO

Building a Data-Driven Culture of Innovation (Chapter 6)
- Re-envisioning Professional Development on Formative Data for All Educators
- Reflecting on the Focus on Summative and Formative Data
- Fostering a Data-Driven Organizational Culture

Formative Data Fosters Educators' Growth Mindset

While formative data points are critical in providing information to meet the needs of each and every student and make the organizational vision more than a talking point, they won't have the desired impact if members of the team do not understand their impact. First, the team must understand how formative data points connect to the development of students' growth mindset. Dweck (2010) explains,

> Individuals with a fixed mindset believe that their intelligence is simply an inborn trait—they have a certain amount, and that's that. In contrast, individuals with a growth mindset believe that they can develop their intelligence over time. (p. 16)

With a growth mindset, students continuously work toward mastery and believe they can learn and grow. Without the belief that they can succeed in areas they are not confident in, how much they can learn is limited, and as such, a vision in which all students are successful cannot come to fruition. In their research, Haimovitz and Dweck (2017) explain,

> These are the first studies we know of that capture how a growth mindset culture may develop through learning-oriented teacher practices (Hooper et al., 2016; Sun, 2015): teaching for understanding, giving feedback that enhances understanding, giving students opportunities to revise their work and display their growing understanding, sending messages about how effort and struggle are part of learning, and scaffolding this message with an emphasis on how teachers will collaborate with students in the learning process. (p. 1855)

The questions we need to ask are:

- How can we ensure that teachers in every classroom reinforce a growth mindset for all students?
- How will our organizational vision inform the steps we take to make fostering students' growth mindset a pivotal element of our instructional program?

Prioritizing growth mindset throughout the organization is closely tied to formative data points since they inform how students are performing and where they need additional support. Therefore, the focus on students' growth mindset must include building educators' capacity to utilize formative data. Nicholson et al. (2017) explains,

> School reform policies and school administrators are increasingly positioning teacher leaders with the responsibility to facilitate evidence-informed conversations with their colleagues that focus on students' learning and lead to effective instructional adjustments. However, teacher leaders need support in learning the new skills and knowledge requisite for successfully facilitating data discussions. For example, learning how to support their colleagues to analyze student evidence and then to translate what they learn into responsive instructional decision making for their classrooms.
> (p. 170)

Consider what professional development is necessary to increase comfort with data analysis and lead to a stronger focus on growth mindset. Use Figure 2.1 to reflect on next steps.

FIGURE 2.1 Connection to Growth Mindset

To what extent is growth mindset encouraged in classrooms throughout the organization? How do you know?	
What specific training opportunities have been offered to foster a growth mindset approach in instruction throughout the district?	
How have conversations about formative assessments connected to growth mindset?	
What supports are needed to build the capacity of all educators to use formative data to enhance students' growth mindset?	

•••

Prioritizing growth mindset throughout the organization is closely tied to formative data points since they inform how students are performing and where they need additional support. Therefore, the focus on students' growth mindset must include building educators' capacity to utilize formative data.

•••

The conversation about real-time formative data must be closely tied to students' growth mindset in order to build their capacity as independent learners. Without this connection, formative data points serve only to inform the teachers' next steps; by including growth mindset, however, students begin to understand their own learning and take more ownership of their educational journey, leading them to become lifelong independent learners. The growth mindset approach transforms students' experience by viewing these data points as a progress check on the way to mastery, a journey that doesn't end until they are successful. As Hattie (2012) explains,

The fundamental premise is that all students should be educated in ways that develop their capability to assess their own learning. So often, the most important decisions tend to be made by adults on behalf of students. Instead, the claim is that the primary function of assessment is to support learning by generating feedback that students can act upon in terms of where they are going, how they are going there, and where they might go next. Such assessment involves active student–teacher collaboration, and teachers who demonstrate that they use assessment in their formative interpretations. (p. 126)

Because of this critical connection between growth mindset and formative data points, serious conversations must take place about data use in the classroom. From their research, Wilkerson et al. (2021) concluded,

Other findings, such as principals perceiving summative and interim data to be more useful than teachers perceive them to be, offer an opportunity to explore why their perceptions differ. Because this study found that teachers' perceptions of and attitudes toward data were positively associated with the actions they reported taking with data, principals' support for professional learning in these areas might be helpful in changing teachers' instructional practice. (p. 12)

As an organization, do all educators make the connections between your vision for serving all students, preparing them to be independent learners by building their growth mindset, and assessing their needs and progress with formative data? If not, consider whether the challenge is a philosophical one or one rooted with disinterest or apprehension with data analysis. If it is the former, you will need to find a way to show educators the power of formative data. If it is the latter, consider conversations using simplified, actionable data points to show their impact on student learning. In both cases, sharing real-life examples of student success can generate interest, passion, and buy-in. Internalizing that there are actual students behind the data is a critical step in generating buy-in.

The growth mindset approach transforms students' experience by viewing these data points as a progress check on the way to mastery, a journey that doesn't end until they are successful.

CONNECTION TO COMPANION BOOK

When used to identify areas of focus and offer supports to address them, formative data can instill a growth mindset in learners. Teachers can use formative data to foster students' growth mindset, and organizational leaders can use formative data to create a culture of learning, growing, and ever-increasing success. In both cases, a developing growth mindset is key to reviewing the data points through the lens of action, improvement, and anticipation for the possibilities they present. Consider how you will develop your team's growth mindset.

Formative data can also impact the growth mindset of educators in departments throughout the district. Team members must believe that the work they are doing will have a genuine impact on student success. While much of the research around growth mindset is focused on students and their belief that they can build mastery in subjects they have not experienced success in, it is also critical to consider the growth mindset of educators. Educators must internalize and believe that they can impact learning, especially for students who have historically struggled. They must also accept that they have the power to impact change. We have all heard reasons why students may be unsuccessful:

students' environment and background, the textbooks chosen by the district, lack of resources, and others. While all may be factors that play a role in student achievement, immediately citing them at the start of the conversation suggests a heavy focus on factors outside of our control instead of taking ownership.

During a data analysis meeting at a school site last year, a group of teachers began discussing students' performance on the math portion of our state assessment. They mentioned the impact of distance learning on student achievement and the benefits of formative assessments to identify students' areas of focus. One teacher added that student success was directly connected to the textbook. The teacher attributed gains to a particular textbook and decreases in performance to another textbook. While the resources available to us certainly play a role in our ability to teach effectively, it was interesting to see the student gains or losses entirely attributed to the textbook. A strong growth mindset acknowledges that resources play a role in student success, but ultimately, our instructional practice plays a tremendous role as well; there is always a way for us to advance learning. A commitment to student learning persuades us to find other resources, strategies, activities, and supports beyond the textbook to ensure student success.

•••

Educators must internalize and believe that they can impact learning, especially for students who have historically struggled. They must also accept that they have the power to impact change.

•••

Just as students' growth mindset development is closely tied to formative data that continuously moves their learning forward, formative feedback for educators can also directly impact their growth mindset. In John Hattie's seminal book *Visible Learning: A Synthesis of Over 800 Meta-Analysis Relating to Achievement*, his research showed that "providing formative evaluation" had a tremendous impact on student achievement with an effect size of d = 0.9 (Hattie, 2009, p. 181). Of the 138 meta-analyses ranked based on impact, "providing formative evaluation" ranked third. For reference, d = 1.0 suggests an increase of one standard deviation in outcome, or advancing student achievement between two and three years (Hattie, 2009, p. 7). With this information, it is clear that formative data is immensely critical to advancing learning and is an essential component of any organizational vision.

Formative Data Informs Planning and Focus Areas

Of course, in addition to developing students' long-term growth mindset, formative data can inform planning and focus areas in the moment. The benefits of formative data points cannot be overemphasized, especially when their impact is maximized using technology. Using data to drive planning seems like a logical step in the organizational growth process, yet it is not as ubiquitous across organizations as it should be, due in large part to the lack of focus, time, commitment, and comfort with the process. Formative data collection, analysis, and structured next steps and timelines must be established to ensure consistent data review and action. A consistent cycle of inquiry such as the Plan-Do-Study-Act (PDSA) cycle must be put in place with a clear focus on targeted areas and how gains will be measured (the PDSA cycle of inquiry will be addressed in greater detail later in this book). The leadership team plays a pivotal role in establishing a culture of inquiry and improvement. Anderson et al. (2010) states, "principals play a key leadership role in establishing the purposes and expectations for data use, structured opportunities (collegial groups and time), data-use training and assistance, access to expertise, and follow-up actions" (p. 323). However, a top-down mandate without buy-in from educators and training will result in half-hearted attempts to look at data until a new focus inevitably comes around and data-driven decision-making fades into the background.

Compounding this challenge is the need to look at data in real-time instead of pulling reports from time to time. New advances and access to technology allow us to examine data "just in time" to maximize their impact, but this now requires additional training as well as a system to easily access real-time data. Think of examples outside your organization in which real-time data can lead to more informed decision-making. Stock prices and traffic information are two examples, and both require easy access to be truly beneficial. Ease of access greatly increases the approachability of the system as well as the time allotted to discussion, feedback, and planning next steps. Just like formative data in the classroom to inform instruction, formative data at the organizational level is only useful if it is tied to feedback and action. Jeong et al. (2020) explains, "For an online-based formative assessment interface, feedback and adaptive assignments are vital aspects that can indicate performance for a diagnostic valuation" (p. 11). Use Figure 2.2 to brainstorm ideas to address the elements required for an effective real-time formative data system. In Part II of this book, we will explore how to build a formative data system for your organization to bring the vision of real-time, data-driven decision-making to life.

FIGURE 2.2 Considerations for Building a Real-Time Formative Data System

Always start with your vision. Restate your organizational vision from Figure 1.2 in this space.	
How much time is regularly devoted to analyzing formative data in your organization?	
What approach do you currently take to implement a cycle of inquiry?	
How do you measure progress?	
What training has your team received on analyzing formative data and planning next steps?	
What supports would you need to incorporate technology regularly to transition to real-time data analysis?	

IMPLEMENTATION TIP

Should the formative data points determine the focus areas, or the focus areas determine the data points? Always begin with the vision and consider the success criteria to support it. Those will help the team narrow down the focus areas, and from there, formative data points can be identified to monitor, evaluate, and act upon. We will examine best practices for pulling and using formative data points to inform next steps for the focus areas later in this book.

At the core of our vision for a data-driven organization is the desire to meet the needs of every student.

TECH TIP

Use visual presentations of formative data and screencasts to bring focus areas to life for the team. Show how the data points connect to focus areas using technology. Visualizations, such as interactive graphs using Power BI (https://powerbi.microsoft.com/en-us/), can facilitate making these connections. Team members can select a focus area and see all the formative data points that apply to it, for example. Making these connections clear helps move the team closer to analyzing the results and discussing next steps.

Formative Data Facilitates Differentiation and Promotes Equity

We know that formative data facilitates growth mindset in the long-term and informs actionable next steps in the short-term, and both of these ultimately serve to provide differentiation to promote equity. At the core of our vision for a data-driven organization is the desire to meet the needs of every student. Think of formative data in the context of a cross-country trip from Los Angeles to New York with students following you in their own cars (this analogy appears in the companion book in a different context—use it or your preferred analogy to impact your team's thinking). You need to arrive in New York with all students, so you will need to check in your rearview mirror often to make sure they are all still following you; these checks are your formative data points. Checking the rearview mirror is not enough, however; if someone is missing, you will need to take action to get them back on the road. The more "real-time" your checks, the less you will need to backtrack and the more effective your supports will be. Equity comes into consideration when different students need different supports. One student may be out of gas, while another may have a flat tire, and yet another may have taken a wrong exit. You'll need to provide differentiated supports—a canister full of gas, a new tire, a navigation system—to make sure each student gets back on the road. A system in place to efficiently provide these supports makes all the difference in how many students make it to New York in a timely manner.

The more "real-time" your checks, the less you will need to backtrack and the more effective your supports will be.

In the classroom, formative data is used to differentiate instruction to meet students' unique needs, but how do formative data points at the organizational level inform differentiation? Should different schools receive differentiated supports? Should organizational-level formative data points continue to offer individualized supports for students? As is often the case, it depends on specific circumstances. A school that is struggling with chronic absenteeism may need to develop a schoolwide plan to address the issue, while a school with few chronically absent students may determine individualized next steps to support them. Formative data points simply provide the information necessary for the team to determine how to proceed with actionable next steps, which can vary greatly depending on the details. Regardless of the decided approach, the ultimate goal is to meet the needs of each individual student behind the data point; that is the equity marker that drives our focus on real-time formative data. As an exercise to inform your thinking, consider a few prominent formative data points in Figure 2.3, and reflect on how you might address them using an inquiry cycle. This exercise will inform your planning steps in Part II.

FIGURE 2.3 Brainstorming How You Might Act on Formative Data

	How will you measure each?	Potential steps if many students are impacted	Potential steps if few students need support	Is there an advantage for having real-time data for this formative data point?	How often will you check for progress for this data point? Why?
Chronic absenteeism					
Graduation rate					
English learner progress					
Mathematics					

FORMATIVE DATA FOR SOCIAL JUSTICE

Formative data analysis is a critical element of designing differentiated supports, which in turn contribute to an equitable vision in which all students succeed. In order to differentiate initiatives and supports at the organizational level, demographic information must be included in the data. Include a wide variety of demographic information in formative data collection, including gender, ethnicity, program participation, language proficiency, socioeconomic status, and more. The platform you use to organize the data should include filters and other tools to disaggregate the data as needed and to identify takeaways that inform next steps. The more demographic information you include, the more useful the data points will be for your team as they will be able to focus on specific student groups and better understand the data. They will also be able to filter for unique groups, such as male English Learners who are Pacific Islander; having the ability to focus on specific groups from the same source data simplifies access and eliminates the need to create multiple data tables for different groups.

Key Takeaways

In this chapter, we built on our new organizational vision by exploring how formative data points can foster educators' growth mindset, inform planning and focus, and ultimately facilitate differentiation and promote equity. Part I of this book has been devoted to understanding the importance of formative data points at the organizational level and exploring how we might maximize their impact through real-time access thanks to technology. In Part II, we will begin developing a plan to bring this vision to life by getting into the details of how to identify critical data points, efficiently collect them, and use best practices to equitably address them.

Part II
Effective Formative Data Use for Leaders

3

Effective Formative Data Use to Drive Organizational Change

Part I: The Need to Reevaluate How We Use Data in Our Organizations

Changing Data Considerations Due to ... (*Introduction*)
♦ Advancements in Technology Changing Formative Data Use
♦ Loss of Consistent Summative Data From Previous Academic Years
♦ Concerns About Data Reliability Due to Limited Measures

Your Organization's Vision and Beliefs (*Chapter 1*)
♦ Assessing Your Organization's Vision
♦ Reflecting on Your Beliefs About Student Learning and Your Role
♦ Where Formative Data Fits In

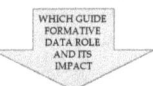

The Impact of Formative Data on Student Success (*Chapter 2*)
♦ Formative Data Fosters Educators' Growth Mindset
♦ Formative Data Informs Planning and Focus Areas
♦ Formative Data Facilitates Differentiation and Promotes Equity

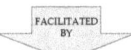

Part II: Effective Formative Data Use for Leaders

Effective Formative Data Use to Drive Organizational Change (*Chapter 3*)	Using Instructional Technology to Effectively Address Formative Data (*Chapter 4*)	Analyzing Formative Data Collaboratively to Identify and Celebrate Best Practices (*Chapter 5*)
♦ How *Actionable* Is the Data You Are Gathering? ♦ How *Timely* Is the Data You Are Gathering? ♦ How Much Data Do You Need? ♦ How Much Time Will It Take to Collect the Data, and Will You Be Able to Address All the Data You Collect?	♦ Efficiently Gathering Formative Data ♦ Identifying and Addressing Validation Concerns to Ensure Broader Impact ♦ Implementing a Collaborative Plan-Do-Study-Act Cycle to Address Data	♦ PLCs using the PDSA cycle ♦ Peer Observations—in-person and virtual ♦ Peer Observations—In-Person and Virtual ♦ Professional Development Linked to Formative Data Page ♦ Including a Wide Variety of Departments to Maximize Perspective and Expertise

Building a Data-Driven Culture of Innovation (*Chapter 6*)
♦ Re-envisioning Professional Development on Formative Data for All Educators
♦ Reflecting on the Focus on Summative and Formative Data
♦ Fostering a Data-Driven Organizational Culture

How *Actionable* Is the Data You Are Gathering?

With our organizational vision intentionally driven by formative data, we are now ready to build a plan to bring it to life. An organization's vision is often viewed as a theoretical end goal we continually strive to reach, and without clear next steps, it will stay firmly as theory. Our students do not have the luxury of a purely theoretical vision, so we must back up our plan with action. Jorno and Gynther (2018) explain that "actionable . . . indicates that analytics is concerned with the potential for practical action rather than either theoretical description or mere reporting" (p. 202). This means starting with a list of next steps:

- Identifying data points to follow that are impactful, actionable, and accessible.
- Determining the inquiry cycle approach to assess progress and iterate as needed.
- Determining the frequency of analysis.
- Creating a system to manage varying inquiry cycles and formative data points to meet the needs of each school.
- Reflecting on their impact for specific students to ensure equity and impact.

The first step may seem easy: choose the data points that appear on your state's summative report and replicate them. California, for example, uses the California State Dashboard (https://caschooldashboard.org/), which reports each year on the following data points: chronic absenteeism, suspension rate, English Learner progress, graduation rate, college/career readiness, English language arts performance, and mathematics performance. The CA dashboard shows progress using data and a five-color system based on a combination of performance and change (red is the lowest, followed by orange, yellow, green, and blue, the highest). Scoring low in a particular metric but showing significant gains compared to the prior year can lead to an improved color assignment. However, there are other data points to consider, such as socioemotional well-being, performance in other subject areas, and Career Technical Education (CTE). Performance for various student stakeholder groups can also be included. Consider which are high priorities in your organization and why they need to be addressed. Be sure to include school sites in the conversation; their input is critical and comes from their insights working directly with students. Schildkamp (2019) explains,

> Important stakeholders in the goal-setting process are school leaders. School leaders need to balance the various goals of different stakeholders with the culture, the vision, mission and values of the school. It is necessary for school leaders to translate policy into the specific goals they think the school should work on: they can prioritise certain goals, and they can influence what data needs to be collected. A key task for school leaders is to make sure that school improvement goals are collectively developed, and that there is dialogue about these goals. (p. 260)

Also, consider their actionability before choosing your formative data points to ensure they will prove useful. It may seem harmless to gather various formative data points and then determine their actionability later, but a potential drawback is a saturation of data which can overwhelm users and potentially distract from the data points that can actually impact student achievement. Additional data points can also take more time to add to your system. It is more effective to choose fewer data points and target your focus on them. To draw a parallel to the formative data use in the classroom we explore in the companion book, *Harnessing Formative Data for K-12 Teachers*, think of a teacher who assigns a dozen math problems to students to assess their mastery levels. The teacher may not have time to carefully review students' work for all 12 problems for a quick turnaround to apply the findings to instruction. By choosing a few problems that are specifically designed to check for understanding and unearth misconceptions, the teacher can maximize the impact of the problems on instruction and apply their takeaways more quickly. Formative assessments that do not inform next steps may take away from instructional time, but formative assessments that inform instruction can add to instructional time by maximizing its effectiveness. The same philosophy can be applied to formative data at the organizational level.

•••

It may seem harmless to gather various formative data points and then determine their actionability later, but a potential drawback is a saturation of data, which can overwhelm users and potentially distract from the data points that can actually impact student achievement.

•••

Fewer data points can also make your formative data viewing system more accessible to users. Team members will have varying comfort levels with analyzing data, and searching through a complex system with multiple submenus and analytics charts can be distracting, especially when several will be passed over because they are informative but not necessarily actionable. Streifer and Schumann (2005) emphasize "the difficulty that school leaders face in using the stores of data they have already collected to analyze the effectiveness of interventions focused on improving achievement" (p. 282). Ensure that users have clear access to the formative data points that will give them the insights needed to inform their next steps. Regardless of your efforts to simplify the data system, training on how to access and interpret the data should be part of your plan. Short screencasts that guide users on how to navigate the system are indispensable and should be included in the training as well as linked on the main access page to increase usage and comfort with the system. You can easily make screencasts using Screencastify, Screencast-o-matic, or any other screencasting program.

The formative system should also be customizable to facilitate looking at the data through different lenses. In the same way that personalized feedback in the classroom can yield better results, customizable formative data can better serve its users. Uribe and Vaughan (2017) explain, "Additional suggestions include personalizing the feedback for the learner, providing frequent and immediate feedback, and asking questions to promote thinking" (p. 289). Different action plans require viewing data in different ways, and this customization functionality will allow users to easily pull the information they need to inform next steps. Researcher Nyland (2018) concludes, "We should place more effort on developing customizable instructor dashboards that present a variety of choices for displaying student data" (p. 522). For example, if the team wants to look at suspension rates for special education students and compare them to rates for general education students, it can do so by simply filtering the results to only show special education students. This is far more effective than generating separate suspension rate data for special education students, general education students, and other stakeholder groups. If the team wants to see the suspension rates for special education students who are also English Learners, a second filter can show this data with one click. You can set up the system to allow this level of customization by adding two elements to each and every formative data point:

- ♦ Add columns of demographic data for each student that is included in the formative data point. These can include school, grade level, ethnicity, English Learner status, socioeconomic level, Gifted and Talented Education program inclusion, and many others.

- Include the ability to sort and filter by each column. This allows users to customize the information displayed for each formative data point to inform next steps to meet their goal.

This approach also facilitates conversations on equity as discrepancies in performance metrics between different stakeholder groups can be easily identified, allowing the majority of time and effort to go to exploring potential reasons for the discrepancies and planning next steps. In our district's formative data system, we automatically display the data for multiple stakeholder groups along with each overall metric result to draw attention to any differences right away. As is the case with any formative data system, our approach does not identify next steps but rather identifies potential areas of focus that require additional exploration and action.

Ease of access is also critical for consistent actionability. If the data points require weeks of gathering from a specialized team, the ability to access them for real-time analysis and action is significantly diminished. To address this concern, we built our formative data system in our student information system (SIS) and included access to it in the very first link at the top left of the screen. This move eliminated the need for users to learn how to use a new site and remember new login information. It also allowed our system to pull the necessary demographic data for customization directly from other sections of the SIS and automatically sync to show any updates, such as additional students enrolling in the district. This system also takes full advantage of advancing technology, requiring less work to access the necessary data after the initial setup. With leaps in data technology use in education in recent years, it is essential to take advantage of their availability to increase ease of access. Dalby and Swan (2019) observe that "the pertinent question to ask is not whether digital technology is being used but how its usage supports teaching and learning" (p. 833).

•••

As is the case with any formative data system, our approach does not identify next steps but rather identifies potential areas of focus that require additional exploration and action.

•••

As you reflect on the best system to develop for your organization, keep in mind the focus of actionable data is student achievement, not accountability. Schildkamp (2019) explains,

> Oftentimes, data are used in a conceptual manner, which means that data use leads to changes into teachers' and school leaders' thinking . . . although this does not necessarily translate into concrete improvement actions. . . . Symbolic data use, misuse and abuse are often consequences of an overly strong focus on accountability instead of on improvement. (p. 266)

•••

🔊 TECH TIP

When designing your formative data platform, include space for identifying potential actions that can be taken to address each data point and include a link to any pertinent templates or resources. Formative data points that do not have any potential actions attached may be temporarily highlighted out until an actionable next step is developed and included. Prioritize actionable data points, and use technology to make this distinction clear.

•••

Any school leader can tell you how easy it is to prioritize accountability over student achievement because accountability is often what is shared with the community. We cannot ignore it but must maintain the perspective that student improvement ultimately yields stronger accountability results.

How *Timely* Is the Data You Are Gathering?

We must also look for ways to make the data points timely to maximize our impact on them. The effective incorporation of technology can dramatically impact the timeliness of the data we access and subsequent action steps they inform. Garcia-Lopez and Garcia-Marazio (2016) explain,

> Over these years of successive innovations, we have observed that increasing the demand of the work throughout the semester has a positive effect on the results. For this ongoing work, timely feedback is vitally important, but this is difficult for the professor to provide, unless tasks are included that can be corrected quickly and/or automatically, with the help of technological tools. (p. 101)

The closer they are to students' day-to-day experiences, the more helpful our efforts will be. Chung et al. (2006) explains,

> The most effective form of assessment is one that is continuous, that occurs as close as possible to the scene of the action in teaching and learning (the classroom), and that provides diagnostic feedback to both teachers and students—to teachers on how they can improve their teaching, to students on how they can improve their learning. (p. 19)

This philosophy applies to data at the organizational level, too.

Let's look at formative data points on graduation rate as an example. Graduation rates are driven by the number of students who complete the required coursework with a passing grade and earn enough credits to graduate. Progress toward graduation updates at the end of each semester or trimester when final course grades are submitted, making it challenging to identify specific factors of the data point to drive timely action. Instead, consider timely factors that ultimately lead to graduation rates and how they can be addressed. One approach is to begin by identifying students who are not on track to graduate by examining completed credits in each year with the credits needed to be on pace for graduation and then looking more closely at those records. Is there a particular course that students are consistently struggling in? Are there specific student stakeholder groups that are disproportionately impacted? What can we learn from schools that show success in these courses? What supports will these students require, and how quickly can we provide them? Drill down to the level of detail required to lead to timely and actionable next steps.

Another example of timely, actionable formative data comes from my experience as an assistant principal at a high school in Inglewood, California. Nearly 93% of the students we served came from socioeconomically disadvantaged backgrounds and often needed targeted supports to be successful. The faculty team included many first-year teachers who were developing their pedagogical craft and required support with effective practices. In addition to offering differentiated training and supports to teachers to build their capacity as educators, the other administrators and I conducted multiple informal observations to gather formative data on instructional practice. Each short observation was followed by a short debrief driven by reflection questions and self-identified actionable next steps. We focused on specific practices each time, uploaded our findings to a shared document to look for patterns and collective areas of growth, and designed schoolwide professional development sessions around instructional practice strategies that would be beneficial to the observed teachers. The professional development sessions modeled classroom best practices, such as differentiation strategies.

Shortly after the trainings, we visited classrooms to check for implementation and debriefed as a team to determine progress and identify next steps. This approach of frequent, short observations followed by training and analysis led to dramatic improvements in instructional practice in only a few months and reinforced the idea that small but consistent steps using formative data were more effective than infrequent, summative data gathering. We learned that extensive observations would yield too much data and would not allow for timely analysis and implementation of next steps. Shorter, informal observations that focused on only one specific strategy led to shorter turnaround times and more meaningful feedback for recent lessons. We eventually expanded this strategy by training the instructional leadership team on providing similar actionable feedback to each other with the ultimate goal of expanding this effort to the entire faculty team. Though the formative data in this example was qualitative, it gave us the information we needed to develop actionable, timely next steps to support student learning.

CONNECTION TO COMPANION BOOK

The meaning of "timely" may differ between data at the organizational level and in the classroom. Formative data points in the classroom should be used to address misconceptions or inform small group planning either the same day or by the next lesson. In contrast, formative data at the organizational level is not addressed within days; rather, it is reviewed and discussed during regularly recurring planning meetings. Schedule these meetings for the year at the start of the school year to ensure consistent analysis.

How Soon Will You Be Able to Act On the Data?

In addition to considering the actionability and timeliness of the data, consider how quickly you will be able to act on the data. Accessing timely data does not necessarily mean you will be able to apply action steps right away. Depending on the particular data point chosen, different factors can impact immediately applicability. Examples include the time of the calendar year, the completion of diagnostic assessments, enrollment cutoff dates, budget timelines, and planned professional development sessions. While taking every possible factor into account can be time-consuming, taking these elements into consideration early on will result in a more robust, meaningful, and effective formative data plan. This in turn will also increase interest and engagement with the formative data system. Knowing that the data analysis will have short-term application increases buy-in, making the actionable steps more likely to be implemented with fidelity.

IMPLEMENTATION TIP

Consider the timing of the formative data you will collect. Data points gathered may be actionable in nature, but if that action cannot take place in a timely manner, their potential impact on student learning will be diminished. Formative data captured around attendance, for example, has a different actionable timeline than formative data points captured on the organization's graduation rate.

How Much Data Do You Need?

As mentioned earlier, it is important to prioritize data that will actually be used. Too much data can distract from the critical data points that inform next steps. Once you determine how you will set up your formative data system, you will have a stronger sense of the effort needed to import real-time data, which in turn can inform how much to start with. Your system will likely go through multiple iterations after users experience it, and additional data points may be added, but it helps to determine a baseline for data import. Discuss options with your team to identify the most critical areas you want to explore using summative data trends you have access to. California users, for example, can use readily available summative data points from multiple sites provided by the California Department of Education, such as the CA Dashboard mentioned earlier, Dataquest (https://data1.cde.ca.gov/dataquest/), and the California Assessment of Student Performance and Progress reporting site (https://caaspp-elpac.cde.ca.gov/caaspp/). Be sure that the data points you are starting with meet the criteria in Figure 2.3 from the previous chapter.

FORMATIVE DATA FOR SOCIAL JUSTICE

In our current data-rich climate, the challenge is often knowing how much data is enough as opposed to struggling to find enough data. To find the right balance, gather enough data to inform supports for multiple subgroups with different needs. If the data available leads to actionable next steps, move forward to ensure students receive supports as soon as possible. The Plan-Do-Study-Act (PDSA) cycle, which we will explore in greater detail in the next chapter, will offer opportunities to reflect on the impact of the supports and help determine if additional data is needed.

How Much Time Will It Take to Collect the Data, and Will You Be Able to Address All the Data You Collect?

Finally, be mindful of how complex it will be to collect the data you plan to analyze. Depending on the focus areas you start with, they may be easily accessed from your SIS to provide real-time data with little effort or may require surveys from stakeholder groups and subsequent formatting for ease of analysis. Do not shy away from exploring data points that require more work to gather and prepare for analysis, but be mindful of the timeline they require to be meaningful to stakeholders and the team. A best practice is to include a variety of quantitative and qualitative formative data points to in order to get the best possible picture of progress and needs. Careful planning will ensure that the more time-consuming data points will be available along with real-time quantitative data during the analysis. Building on your reflection in Figure 2.3, use Figure 3.1 to identify formative data points you will include in your system and determine the ideal timing, potential actionability, level of detail, and effort involved to collect the data.

TECH TIP

As you list topic areas you will collect data points for, include space to identify frequency of collection. For example, attendance can be captured daily, while math results from interim assessments may be captured monthly. If possible, include links to the reports directly on the page and include recurring calendar meeting-makers to team members who will compile the data. The more this process is clearly laid out and streamlined at the start, the more prepared participants will be to analyze the data points instead of spending time locating them.

FIGURE 3.1 Beginning Steps of Developing Your Formative Data System

Data point to include	How it can lead to action	What level of detail is needed	Most effective time of year for initial review	Complexity involved in gathering this data point

CONNECTION TO COMPANION BOOK

The companion book explains that formative assessments can impact instructional time, so any time devoted to them must serve to inform and improve instruction. Formative assessments that include prompts that do not inform next steps can negatively impact achievement because they took time away from learning without contributing insights to learning. Similarly, formative data points at the organizational level must lead to actionable next steps. Only collect data points you will analyze and address because time spent gathering additional data that goes unused can take away from other district priorities.

Do not shy away from exploring data points that require more work to gather and prepare for analysis, but be mindful of the timeline they require to be meaningful to stakeholders and the team.

Key Takeaways

In this chapter, we explored how to identify formative data points that can lead to action, determine the level of detail that may be needed, choose the most effective timeline for analysis, and consider the complexity involved in gathering the data. We now have all the pieces to begin the actual development of a real-time formative data system to efficiently analyze data that can have a direct impact on student achievement. In the next chapter, we will examine different programs you can use to develop and house your formative data system. Every organization will have different access to systems that can work depending on the SIS they use, the technical expertise their team possesses, and the resources available; fortunately, a well-designed system will provide the necessary data regardless of platform. Use this opportunity to push the boundaries of innovation and see what technologies are at your disposable to make the best possible system to serve students.

4

Using Instructional Technology to Effectively Address Formative Data

Part I: The Need to Reevaluate How We Use Data in Our Organizations

Changing Data Considerations Due to . . . (Introduction)
♦ Advancements in Technology Changing Formative Data Use
♦ Loss of Consistent Summative Data From Previous Academic Years
♦ Concerns About Data Reliability Due to Limited Measures

NECESSITATE NEED TO REVISIT VISION

Your Organization's Vision and Beliefs (Chapter 1)
♦ Assessing Your Organization's Vision
♦ Reflecting on Your Beliefs About Student Learning and Your Role
♦ Where Formative Data Fits In

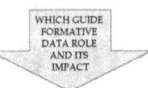

WHICH GUIDE FORMATIVE DATA ROLE AND ITS IMPACT

The Impact of Formative Data on Student Success (Chapter 2)
♦ Formative Data Fosters Educators' Growth Mindset
♦ Formative Data Informs Planning and Focus Areas
♦ Formative Data Facilitates Differentiation and Promotes Equity

FACILITATED BY

Part II: Effective Formative Data Use for Leaders

Effective Formative Data Use to Drive Organizational Change (Chapter 3)	Using Instructional Technology to Effectively Address Formative Data (Chapter 4)	Analyzing Formative Data Collaboratively to Identify and Celebrate Best Practices (Chapter 5)
♦ How *Actionable* Is the Data You Are Gathering? ♦ How *Timely* Is the Data You Are Gathering? ♦ How Much Data Do You Need? ♦ How Much Time Will It Take to Collect the Data, and Will You Be Able to Address All the Data You Collect?	♦ Efficiently Gathering Formative Data ♦ Identifying and Addressing Validation Concerns to Ensure Broader Impact ♦ Implementing a Collaborative Plan-Do-Study-Act Cycle to Address Data	♦ PLCs using the PDSA cycle ♦ Peer Observations—In-Person and Virtual ♦ Professional Development Linked to Formative Data Page ♦ Including a Wide Variety of Departments to Maximize Perspective and Expertise

WHICH WILL LEAD TO

Building a Data-Driven Culture of Innovation (Chapter 6)
♦ Re-envisioning Professional Development on Formative Data for All Educators
♦ Reflecting on the Focus on Summative and Formative Data
♦ Fostering a Data-Driven Organizational Culture

In our data-rich environment, looking at data points through a critical lens and identifying ones that are actionable will lead to more impactful supports and initiatives and ultimately greater student success. In the previous chapter, your team collaboratively identified data points that would be actionable and timely; we must now review the logistical considerations to make gathering them on a regular basis efficient and manageable. Formative data by nature must be reviewed more than once, so the systems we design to pull the data must be easy to utilize repeatedly. In this chapter, we will explore strategies for developing a comprehensive formative data gathering system and the foundation for collaborative analysis and action.

Efficiently Gathering Formative Data

Many years ago, I read about a study in which two groups of participants were given a plate of cookies and asked not to eat them. One group was given math problems to work on while waiting, and the other group was not. Over time, the participants in the group who were working on the math problems began to eat the cookies. The researchers' conclusion was that the finite amount of perseverance participants had was partially depleted by the effort required to do the problems, leading to a greater willingness to take a cookie. A similar pattern can unfold if the formative data points we need to access take excessive time and effort to access: the finite amount of time and energy we have will go to gathering the data, leaving little of each for analysis and planning actionable next steps. This sequence is particularly easy to replicate at school site trainings with limited windows for collaboration and professional development; if 45 minutes of an hour-long meeting are devoted to accessing formative data, how much will our students be impacted by the analysis and planning that occurs in the remaining 15 minutes? To maximize the impact of real-time formative data on student achievement, we must make access painless and analysis rich. The recommendations that follow are designed to do just that.

Systematize as Much as Possible

First, use your existing data systems as much as possible. This eliminates the need for users to learn new programs and remember more websites and login credentials. It also cuts down on the data syncing requirements between your SIS and other programs and minimizes your organization's data exposure, ensuring the highest possible level of data privacy. In our district, we worked with our SIS provider and created a formative version of the California State Dashboard in our SIS to give us real-time data on student success in a variety of metrics. Unlike the state dashboard, which serves as a summative report for the entire year, our internal formative version shows us progress toward mastery *throughout* the year. In addition to providing subgroup performance in each metric as the state dashboard does, our formative dashboard also shows the students who comprise each subgroup so we know who needs additional support in each metric. Of course, we also use other formative data points outside of the CA dashboard metrics such as socioemotional data.

We got started by thinking about how we could get the greatest amount of buy-in from stakeholders and determined that developing an initial system aligned to the state dashboard would be instantly recognized and understood by stakeholders. The system would provide data on the same metrics, albeit as formative data. We contacted our SIS vendor to see if we could build a formative data system within the program by pulling data available in the system. The undertaking would be particularly tricky because the state dashboard we wanted to model our system after used complex formulas and tables to measure progress by taking into account both performance and change compared to the prior year. After a few discussions regarding feasibility and design, the vendor and our IT team set out to collaboratively build the system. We set requirements to maximize the actionability of the system:

- Use as much real-time data as possible using updated information from our SIS.
- Make the system easy to access and use.
- Include multiple student stakeholder groups automatically for each data metric to show comparisons.
- Allow users to drill down to the student level with one click so we could quickly identify the individual students who comprised the data point.
- Allow for spreadsheet export to allow further customization and analysis as needed.

Some data points such as chronic absenteeism rates and suspension rates relied on real-time data from the SIS, while others required formulas to track progress. The college/career readiness metric, for example, used formulas to determine progress based on completed coursework, CTE pathway completion, and other metrics. Yet others relied on formative assessments provided by teachers; English language arts and mathematics formative data calculations, for example, were made based on interim assessments teachers provided. The results were regularly exported to the system to provide the most up-to-date data. While the system is far from perfect, it provides district and school leaders with critical, timely information to inform next steps. Whenever possible, the formative data provided is real-time to maximize its effectiveness. Check with your SIS team to see if a dashboard that houses formative data can be added to your account. As much as possible, keep your formative data reports in your SIS to make access easy. An additional benefit to this approach is the reduced opportunities for outdated or incorrect data to end up in the formative data review meetings. Discovering that the team has been using inaccurate data can lead to frustration if time and energy was spent reviewing it, and skepticism about the data points can arise in future meetings, which can distract from the purpose of the meetings.

TECH TIP

As much as possible, choose an option that capitalizes on syncing with your SIS to minimize the likelihood of accidentally viewing outdated data. A data visualization system that regularly syncs with the SIS consistently offers real-time data without the need for manual calculations and multiple data file management. It yields better results and requires less work to get them. Do not hesitate to conduct extensive research on options that include syncing when initially setting up your system; the effort will be worthwhile.

If this is not possible at this time, consider other options. You can create and save reports in your SIS that can be run by any user. You can also link reports like attendance and discipline incidents to Power BI (https://powerbi.microsoft.com/en-us/), a powerful data visualization program from Microsoft that allows users to view data points in graphs and charts that can easily be manipulated through filters and other adjustments. In addition to aiding understanding, the Power BI data visualizations can be linked to data files and automatically update with changing data. Another option to consider is an educational data and assessment program such as Illuminate (www.illuminateed.com/), which has several reports already developed and available and syncs directly to the SIS. Using a program like Illuminate does not require programming expertise, but the options for report types and details may also be more limited.

Keep your formative data reports in your SIS to make access easy. An additional benefit to this approach is the reduced opportunities for outdated or incorrect data to end up in the formative data review meetings.

CONNECTION TO COMPANION BOOK

In addition to providing data reports that can be used to review formative data, Illuminate also offers a formative assessment development tool that facilitates collaborative assessment development and analysis. The tool allows teachers to choose from a vast library of standards-based questions or to include their own questions in a formative assessment. The companion discusses this resource in greater detail.

You may also consider using pivot tables in Microsoft Excel to view consolidated data from raw report files, but you will need to run a new report and take the steps to summarize the data each time. Depending on the topic, the size of the file, and the steps required to create actionable pivot tables, this option can take more time to utilize than the others. As your team considers its approach, keep in mind that the formative data pull must be replicated several times each year with ease; if the process is overly cumbersome, data analysis meetings may lose their effectiveness over time. Using an offline program such as Excel also increases the possibility of losing data due to an unsaved file or juggling multiple versions of the file as well as limiting collaboration by only allowing one person to access the file at a time. If your team determines that Microsoft Excel is the most appropriate tool, consider uploading the file to a cloud-based service such as Microsoft's online Office suite or Google's Sheets app (with proper data security measures in place of course).

Make the Data Easy to Access

In addition to increasing efficiency, easy access to the data also contributes to building trust within the organization. When the team is willing to look critically at the data and have frank conversations about focus areas worth celebrating and those that need more support, it sends a clear message to all members that they are trusted with the data and are collectively responsible for advancing student progress.

Several key practices can make the data more accessible. First, all data points should be organized on one site or document to eliminate unnecessary searching or frustration. Even if the data points are pulled from different resources, links to each can appear on the document. You may consider adding an intranet page to your organization's website that is password-protected or a Google Docs page with links. It will be helpful to make an easy-to-remember shortcut to the page using sites such as www.bitly.com or www.tinyurl.com. Next, make a short screencast for each data point in which you show users how to access the data points and include a brief tour of the features for that source, such as how to filter for specific subgroups. Two options to consider are https://screencast-o-matic.com/ and www.screencastify.com/. Both are highly effective and easy to use.

TECH TIP

Screencasts are incredibly helpful tools for guiding users through new websites, processes, and programs. Use them often, and include hyperlinks to them when sending messages about new resources. They can dramatically lessen the number of technical questions and create more engagement with resources. Keep the screencasts short—with few exceptions, they should be limited to under four minutes. Longer screencasts tend to have fewer viewers, so keep the recordings short and sweet. You can make several short screencasts instead of one long one to eliminate the need for users to search through the video looking for the part they need. This approach also reduces the need to rerecord long videos if an error forces a restart. The screencasts do not need to be high production videos with fancy graphics additions or editing; as long as they clearly communicate the required steps, they are acceptable.

Ensure that these easily accessible data points are available and applicable to critical stakeholders in your organization. You can engage stakeholders and make the data points applicable by including several demographic fields in all data points, allowing easy filtering by one or more areas. Including special education designation can engage the Special Education department in the data points, for example. Other demographic fields to consider include English language proficiency, ethnicity, gender, grade level, and socioeconomic status. Be sure to limit access to demographic information based on current state and federal guidelines. For data points based on occurrences such as attendance or

FIGURE 4.1 Demographic Data to Include

Demographic Field to Include	Reason for Inclusion

disciplinary instances, consider including the day of the week in addition to the date, which may help identify trends and inform initiatives. Use Figure 4.1 to identify demographic info you will include in your formative data files.

•••

When the team is willing to look critically at the data and have frank conversations about focus areas worth celebrating and those that need more support, it sends a clear message to all members that they are trusted with the data and are collectively responsible for advancing student progress.

•••

Identifying and Addressing Validation Concerns to Ensure Broader Impact

Gathering real-time formative data efficiently is a critical step in identifying actionable next steps to address areas of focus, but it will only benefit the process if users trust the validity of the data. If the data is dismissed as inaccurate, incomplete, or misleading, users will naturally revert to decision-making based on other factors. The data page must be trusted in terms of its accuracy and its applicability to measurable success criteria.

One way to address this concern is to present the data using the same metrics as the summative state data—so long as the data points are actionable. This minimizes potential discussions on why the data points are calculated as they are and instead prioritizes reflecting on their implications and next steps. The focus of data analysis must always be on actionable next steps to support students. In our district, we used the same color band system based on performance and improvement from the prior year that the state used for certain data points, such as chronic absenteeism rate, and this decision contributed to the validity of our numbers, especially when questions about the inner workings of the calculations came up (such as how many days a student must attend a school before being included in the count). Unlike the summative results released by the state each year, our formative data system allowed users to click on the count of students comprising a particular percentage and see the names of the students who comprise the count. This dramatically increased the potential for actionable next steps as users were able to identify *students* who need additional support, not only subgroups.

Also, be sure to take into account the student size of the data points in order to accurately portray trends. Show both percentage and count whenever possible. For example, if the percentage of students suspended in a particular subgroup dramatically jumps in a single quarter due to the small size of the subgroup, it would be helpful to note that the subgroup is very small and therefore can have larger fluctuations.

FORMATIVE DATA FOR SOCIAL JUSTICE

Subgroups with a small number of students may be more easily missed because of their perceived limited impact on the overall student success of the organization. The students in those subgroups, however, are often the most at-risk and need support. For this reason, be sure to include smaller subgroups on the same plane as larger subgroups, and include percentages as well as numbers. Remind the team that successful interventions and initiatives that impact smaller subgroups can inform supports for other subgroups, and, most importantly, that we must serve all students if we are championing social justice.

Include footnotes whenever possible for anticipated questions about the data. If data points are missing for a particular term and the report references older data points instead for one of the focus areas, include a message explaining this before the question arises. This transparency serves to reinforce trust in

FIGURE 4.2 Data Points to Use for Measuring Progress

Data Point	Source	How It Is Actionable	Lead Departments/ Personnel	Notes

the data and minimizes logistical questions, allowing the team to focus on next steps instead. Once again, the goal is to limit challenges with accessing and understanding the data to maximize the time and effort spent on addressing the data. A lot of thought and planning must go into creating the data documents with links, footnotes, descriptions, and screencasts, but the initial investment in time and effort will pay dividends once the year is underway and the leadership team is able to access and analyze with ease multiple times each semester.

With these elements in place, we now have a comprehensive formative data source that we will revisit on a regular basis to monitor progress and adjust supports as needed. Use Figure 4.2 to draft what your formative data page will look like.

Implementing a Collaborative Plan-Do-Study-Act Cycle to Address Data

With data points identified and logistics for easy access in place, we are ready to begin exploring the process for analysis and action. A powerful approach for analysis and change is the Plan-Do-Study-Act (PDSA) cycle, which guides data users through data analysis, a plan of action, checking progress, and making adjustments to the plan as necessary. Originally developed by W. Edwards Deming (Moen & Norman, 2010, p. 26) and refined over the years, the PDSA cycle provides "a manageable and timely way for teachers to study the impact of their practice and to take ownership of the solutions that they developed" (Fatout, 2015, p. 14) and is built around the concept of regularly measured formative data analysis. Researchers MacLeod et al. (2019) conclude, "The cycle is a perfect symbol for a continual improvement system as each step leads to the next" (p. 59). In this chapter, we will develop a foundation for using the PDSA cycle, while the next chapter will go into the details for collaborative implementation. Figure 4.3 shows the PDSA cycle and the actions to undertake at each step. These steps should be followed regardless of the team leading this work or the data points the team is focusing on. It should also be emphasized that the PDSA cycle is a formative data analysis process that promotes growth mindset as areas of focus are identified and strategies for improvement are implemented, especially when it is used "to encourage students to plan to achieve small goals that can help other larger goals to actualize" (Sears et al., 2019, p. 898). Any data analysis process should employ some iteration of the PDSA cycle.

Your team should set recurring meetings at the start of the year to monitor progress throughout the year. Trying to align calendars to schedule these meetings during the year may be challenging and may lead to breaks in the PDSA cycle, which can impact the effectiveness of the initiatives designed to address focus areas. Ideally, these meetings will take place at least monthly to monitor progress and address concerns in a timely manner. There must be a sense of urgency around addressing the data points; our students deserve rapid response to their needs to ensure their success. Also, note "that cycles occur rather quickly. Small changes are made, data are quickly and easily gathered, and these data inform the next steps. The overarching

FIGURE 4.3 The Plan-Do-Study-Act Cycle

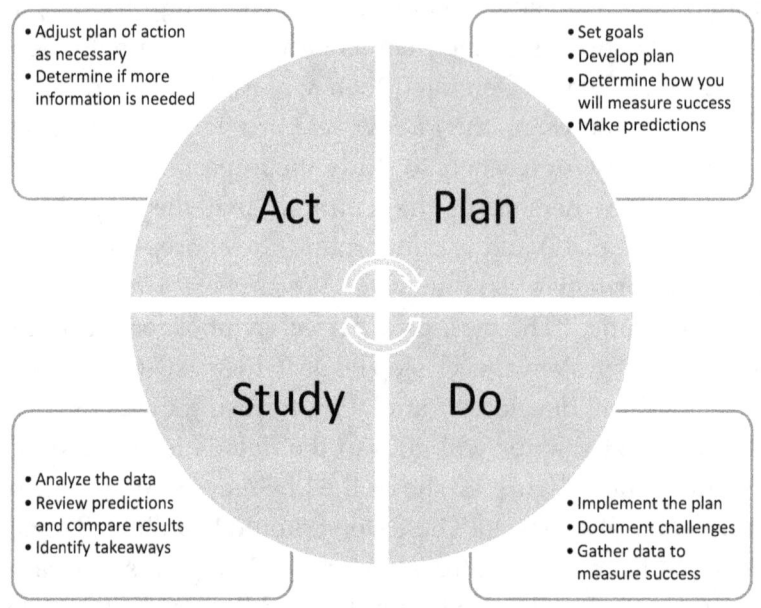

CONNECTION TO COMPANION BOOK

The PDSA cycle is a critical element of the formative data analysis process at the organizational level, but it is more difficult to consistently execute at the classroom level. Teachers use a combination of on-the-fly and planned formative assessments to inform instruction and interventions and require a faster version of the cycle. Formative data must be analyzed and acted upon on the same day or the next lesson in order to be timely and applicable to the learning process. This timeline also necessitates shortened formative assessments to minimize time taken from instruction and maximize actionable next steps. At both levels, however, formative data collection must be strictly focused on direct impact to student achievement; data points that do not inform planning should be secondary.

goal may be ambitious. However, the changes made in each cycle should be small, attainable, and easily measurable" (Rowland et al., 2018, p. 36).

In the Plan stage of the cycle, the team meets to set goals, develop a plan, and determine how they will measure success using a variety of data points that will be monitored. The team also makes predictions to set a baseline for expectations. In the Do stage of the cycle, the team implements the developed plan and gathers data to assess progress. The team also documents challenges faced along the way to inform the analysis and potential update to the plan. After implementation, the team analyzes the data, reflects on the predictions, and assesses progress toward success. Act, the final stage of the cycle, adjusts the plan of action if necessary to inform the planning stage of the next cycle. Repeating this cycle with thoughtful planning and implementation yields consistently improving outcomes as the supports, interventions, and initiatives developed by the team become more refined and better target focus areas.

IMPLEMENTATION TIP

Consider how you will organize your data review meetings to facilitate streamlined access to the findings from last time and how this round compares. Details on the actions implemented in the last round of the PDSA cycle and their impact should be readily available and set up in a format that can easily be compared to the current round. The clearer the access and process, the more the focus will be on the critical conversations stemming from the data. Consider having one link for all materials with sections for the different rounds; two options are an online sheet with tabs for each round or a website with a page devoted to each round.

There must be a sense of urgency around addressing the data points; our students deserve rapid response to their needs to ensure their success.

FIGURE 4.4 Plan-Do-Study-Act Planning Template

	Plan			Do	Study		Act	
Session #	Goal	Plan to achieve goal	How you will measure success	Prediction	Challenges faced during implementation	Prediction outcome	Takeaway	Any adjustments?	More info needed?

In the spirit of simplifying access to data and eliminating logistical hurdles in order to maximize time for analysis and planning next steps, a digital version of the PDSA graphic in Figure 4.3 should be used with hyperlinks to relevant documents to aid analysis. For example, the "Gather data to measure success" bullet should be hyperlinked with the data source page summarized in Figure 4.2. Similarly, the analysis tool used by the team should be linked to "Analyze the data." By creating one document to guide the process, your team will quickly access critical information, make connections between various steps, and more efficiently reach actionable planning phase. You may use Figure 4.4 to jot notes on the PDSA cycle to aid in planning.

Key Takeaways

In this chapter, we reviewed how to plan your team's approach for effectively using technology to gather and analyze real-time formative data. By creating systems that minimize logistical challenges and keep the focus on actionable next steps, your team will be able to regularly review progress toward established goals in a transparent format that fosters trust and inclusivity and take advantage of the expertise of a variety of departments and practitioners. In the next chapter, we will explore how the PDSA cycle can be used collaboratively to build capacity and greater understanding of students' successes and needs. The impact of the PDSA cycle will be felt once collaborative teams begin using it to discuss best practices and consistently hone the instructional program.

5

Analyzing Formative Data Collaboratively to Identify and Celebrate Best Practices

Part I: The Need to Reevaluate How We Use Data in Our Organizations

Changing Data Considerations Due to ... *(Introduction)*
♦ Advancements in Technology Changing Formative Data Use
♦ Loss of Consistent Summative Data From Previous Academic Years
♦ Concerns About Data Reliability Due to Limited Measures

Your Organization's Vision and Beliefs *(Chapter 1)*
♦ Assessing Your Organization's Vision
♦ Reflecting on Your Beliefs About Student Learning and Your Role
♦ Where Formative Data Fits In

The Impact of Formative Data on Student Success *(Chapter 2)*
♦ Formative Data Fosters Educators' Growth Mindset
♦ Formative Data Informs Planning and Focus Areas
♦ Formative Data Facilitates Differentiation and Promotes Equity

Part II: Effective Formative Data Use for Leaders

Effective Formative Data Use to Drive Organizational Change *(Chapter 3)*	Using Instructional Technology to Effectively Address Formative Data *(Chapter 4)*	Analyzing Formative Data Collaboratively to Identify and Celebrate Best Practices *(Chapter 5)*
♦ How *Actionable* Is the Data You Are Gathering? ♦ How *Timely* Is the Data You Are Gathering? ♦ How Much Data Do You Need? ♦ How Much Time Will It Take to Collect the Data, and Will You Be Able to Address All the Data You Collect?	♦ Efficiently Gathering Formative Data ♦ Identifying and Addressing Validation Concerns to Ensure Broader Impact ♦ Implementing a Collaborative Plan-Do-Study-Act Cycle to Address Data	♦ PLCs using the PDSA cycle ♦ Peer Observations—In-Person and Virtual ♦ Professional Development Linked to Formative Data Page ♦ Including a Wide Variety of Departments to Maximize Perspective and Expertise

Building a Data-Driven Culture of Innovation *(Chapter 6)*
♦ Re-envisioning Professional Development on Formative Data for All Educators
♦ Reflecting on the Focus on Summative and Formative Data
♦ Fostering a Data-Driven Organizational Culture

Analyzing Formative Data Collaboratively ◆ 81

With a formative data system in place and a Plan-Do-Study-Act cycle of inquiry ready to go, we are now ready to explore practices to act on the actionable data. As you work with your team to determine the next steps you will take to address the data, ask if they require resources, professional development, a policy update, or a combination of the three. Regardless of approach, meaningful and lasting success can only come from a collaboration effort from departments, schools, and community members who all prioritize achievement for all students.

••

It is only a steadfast commitment to ***every single student*** that will allow us to truly reach our vision of equity. This commitment must drive our actions, and the leadership team must espouse it publicly and often.

••

In this chapter, we will examine how to use the cycle of inquiry to analyze the formative data we have collected to meet the needs of *every* student. Before we begin, keep in mind that resources, professional development, and policies will likely meet the needs of *many* students, but it is only a steadfast commitment to *every single student* that will allow us to truly reach our vision of equity. This commitment must drive our actions, and the leadership team must espouse it publicly and often. I was lucky enough to work on a team with an incredible superintendent and assistant superintendent, both of whom consistently emphasized the importance of considering every student. If an action step proposed would meet the needs of 999 out of 1,000 students, they would ask how we could serve the other student. This steadfast push for equity took extra time and effort, but it is precisely this level of commitment to equity that ensures that marginalized students do not "slip through the cracks" of the education system, to borrow a popular phrase. Seeing how much additional focus is necessary to ensure equity reveals why it is so easy to forget about the students who will be left behind. With an effective, real-time formative data system, a commitment to equity, and a powerful vision driving your work, you will go beyond catching students before they slip through the cracks: you will fill those cracks until they get smaller and smaller until they have all but disappeared in your organization. As DuFour (2004) explains,

> School mission statements that promise "learning for all" have become a cliché. But when a school staff takes that statement literally—when teachers view it as a pledge to ensure the success of each student rather than as politically correct hyperbole—profound changes begin to take place.

Those changes require a clear plan for reviewing formative data points and taking action based on them, and this chapter highlights several ways your team can make that practice a cornerstone of your organizational vision.

....

With an effective, real-time formative data system, a commitment to equity, and a powerful vision driving your work, you will go beyond catching students before they slip through the cracks: you will fill those cracks until they get smaller and smaller until they have all but disappeared in your organization.

....

PLCs Using the PDSA Cycle

As discussed in the companion book, Professional Learning Communities (PLCs) are teams of educators who meet on a regular basis to discuss instruction, engage in cycles of inquiry, and collaboratively look at student data. PLCs were popularized by Richard DuFour and continue to be among the more popular formats for cycles of inquiry. Cycles of inquiry are intertwined with formative data analysis; regularly checking for and reflecting on progress are essential for success. McKay et al. (2020) states,

> Continuous feedback loops, including the use of external evaluators, are also necessary to ensure that stakeholder concerns can be identified and addressed in a timely manner. Such responsiveness further enhances a sense of trust and ownership in the created organization and bodes well for its ongoing success. (p. 3)

It is important to note, however, that cycles of inquiry are only effective if action steps take place between data review meetings. For example, if you have set a weight loss goal and decide to check your weight every two weeks, you will need to take certain steps in between weigh-ins to see change. Weighing yourself more frequently doesn't bring you closer to your goal: the action steps you take make the difference. If you see success, you can reflect on what steps you took and why they were effective and may make further updates if needed. If you did not see the change you hoped for, you can make adjustments before the next check. It can be challenging, especially if you are not sure if the steps you are taking will lead to your desired outcome.

Now imagine if you had a partner working toward the same goal as you, experienced similar challenges, and shared strategies that were successful. Together, you have encouragement, insight, collaboration, and a common purpose. Hord (1997, p. 14) shares some of the attributes of effective professional learning communities, including supportive and shared leadership, collective creativity, shared values and vision, supportive conditions, and shared personal practice. These all play a part in a successful PLC model. The following critical elements must be present for a PLC model to be successful:

- A clear vision and goals for the PLC.
- A culture of collaboration and innovation.
- Clear steps for data analysis, including what to look for and the data-driven decision-making that follows.

DuFour (2004) brings these three elements together using three questions, explaining,

When the staff has built shared knowledge and found common ground on these questions, the school has a solid foundation for moving forward with its improvement initiative.

- What do we want each student to learn?
- How will we know when each student has learned it?
- How will we respond when a student experiences difficulty in learning?

The answer to the third question separates learning communities from traditional schools.

Notice the word "each" come up more than once in his questions. The focus here is on ensuring every single student's success, and that can only come from being aware of their needs and addressing them in a timely manner. Unpacking these questions through the lens of formative data shows that data analysis is critical to answering them:

- *What do we want each student to learn?*—This question requires a clear organizational vision on what student learning looks like in classrooms and what learning objectives the organization prioritizes.
- *How will we know when each student has learned it?*—This question clearly focuses on formative and summative data that aligns to the objectives identified in the first question. Summative assessments alone may show student

mastery levels, but any gaps in student learning may be hard to address using the third question because of the amount of content covered in the summative assessment and the limited timeliness of the action steps. Formative assessments are key to answering this question.
- *How will we respond when a student experiences difficulty in learning?*—This question focuses on the actionable next steps that come from the data analysis. These are the critical supports we provide to ensure *each* student is successful. When we respond in a timely manner, we are much more likely to see the positive impact of our efforts by providing supports when they are needed the most and when the student is most likely to take advantage of them.

DuFour (2004) emphasizes that these supports stemming from the formative data must be:

- *Timely*. The school quickly identifies students who need additional time and support.
- *Based on intervention rather than remediation*. The plan provides students with help as soon as they experience difficulty rather than relying on summer school, retention, and remedial courses.
- *Directive*. Instead of inviting students to seek additional help, the systematic plan requires students to devote extra time and receive additional assistance until they have mastered the necessary concepts.

We see the potential impact of a well-conceived PLC model, but bringing it to life for your team requires more than just introducing the idea. Participants must be on board with the vision that targets all students and be committed to regularly revisiting the data points and implementing action steps between them. An established cycle of inquiry can help facilitate the data analysis conversations in PLCs and one of the most effective is the Plan-Do-Study-Act (PDSA) cycle you developed in Figure 4.4 in the previous chapter. You can use your PLC to review data and next steps using the PDSA cycle. The PLC provides the vision, space, and team to focus on student outcomes, while the PDSA cycle offers an approach to make the PLC discussions meaningful and actionable. DuFour also emphasizes the importance of focusing on results, which can be assessed by observing formative data over time. Use Figure 5.1 to begin developing the framework for your PLC team, including how the PDSA cycle will guide the conversation.

IMPLEMENTATION TIP

The PDSA cycle is a powerful approach to consistently analyze real-time formative data points, determine next steps, and assess the effectiveness of the action plan. However, not all team members may be familiar with the process or its best practices. Consider how you will introduce the PDSA cycle in your PLCs. In addition to starting with an introductory message, sharing success stories and going through a few rounds of the PDSA cycle can help increase familiarity and buy-in.

As you discuss potential action steps, it may be helpful to identify specific students who may benefit from them. This reinforces the fact that there are students behind the data points, and they may need a host of different supports to be successful. One course of action may not be enough to ensure their success. Each student has different needs, and it is critical to understand the whole child to fulfill an organizational vision based on equity and social justice.

Technology can enhance this work by helping track progress on the focus areas of the PLC. Videoconferencing can help move the efforts of the PLC forward when meeting in person proves challenging. Technology can also expedite analysis using collaborative documents that several participants can work on simultaneously, adding insights, comments, and data points.

FIGURE 5.1 Your PLC Framework

PLAN: Which data point(s) will your PLC target?	
PLAN: How does this data point advance your organizational vision from Figure 1.3?	
PLAN: How often will you meet as part of your cycle of inquiry?	
PLAN: Describe any specific roles PLC members will play and why.	
DO: How will technology help facilitate: ♦ **Data collection** ♦ **Data analysis** ♦ **Putting next steps into action**	
STUDY: How will you measure student access for this data point? Describe the evidence the team will bring to the PLC.	
ACT: What process will you use to determine actionable next steps based on the presented outcomes?	

Incorporate technology in your PLC efforts to maximize its impact and timeliness.

•••

We usually think of classroom instruction when we think of peer observations, but we have peers in a variety of roles in an organization who are doing great work and willing to share their practices.

•••

Peer Observations—In-Person and Virtual

Another powerful approach to support actionable next steps on data is to employ peer observations throughout the district. We usually think of classroom instruction when we think of peer observations, but we have peers in a variety of roles in an organization who are doing great work and willing to share their practices. Peer observations require planning, time, coverage arrangements, and other considerations, which may limit how often it is used in organizations. However, the benefits of peer observations are so vast that the effort to arrange them is certainly worth it. When I helped launch a districtwide blended learning training program, participants frequently mentioned how well they understood the concepts explored in the professional development sessions because of the peer observations we included in the learning. They also shared how observations helped accelerate their application of the strategies in the training sessions, especially when they were able to debrief with the teachers they observed. With our newfound comfort with videoconferencing, some observations can also be done virtually depending on the focus area. Logistics can be worked out if your team is willing to prioritize the observations.

First, you must establish the potential benefits of peer observations for your team and get buy-in. This means the team must believe that the observations will yield actionable next steps that can be implemented at your site. The team must start with the collective

TECH TIP

Peer observations involve considerable logistical planning, especially when observing teachers at other schools. A few years ago, the thought of virtual observations using videoconferencing technology may have seemed far-fetched; after the pandemic-driven distance learning experience, however, using videoconferencing for observations seems far more plausible. If in-person observations are not possible due to scheduling or distance, consider virtual observations instead. Classrooms equipped with cameras as part of the transition from distance to hybrid learning may be particularly welcoming to virtual observations.

FIGURE 5.2 Establishing Buy-In for Organizational Peer Observation

Describe your team's current belief regarding peer observations.	
How can you know if your team believes that observation takeaways can apply to your organization?	
Has your team conducted peer observations both in and out of the classroom in the past? Why or why not?	
If not, what has held the team back?	
How will you address it?	

belief that all students can succeed and that we can impact all students' success. You may have to address comments about how "our students are different" and that the lessons learned from observation will not apply to your organization. Until this buy-in is established, any potential takeaway from the observations will be diminished. Use Figure 5.2 to plan how you will establish this collective buy-in.

Once your team is ready, look back at your data points and determine how peer observations can inform next steps that can be shared in PLCs. Different types of observations can provide insight for different data points. Here are a few examples:

Focus Area	Potential Observation Plan
Chronic absenteeism	Schedule an observation with a principal at a school that has lowered its chronic absenteeism rate through a series of initiatives such as parent/guardian outreach and effective School Attendance Review Board (SARB) implementation.
Low 9th grade math scores	Schedule an observation at a school that has developed a system for assessing incoming student areas of strength and growth and implementing differentiated instruction to meet the needs of each student. Observe school site professional development on the topic and classroom instruction to see how the differentiation is implemented.

Focus Area	Potential Observation Plan
Dropout rates	Observe a school that has developed a system for effectively supporting at-risk students through interactions with counselors, differentiated support, and parent/guardian outreach.
Suspension rates	Observe leaders in a school who have adopted a plan to lower their suspension rates through a combination of targeted school culture development, restorative practices, and parent/guardian outreach.

While every school community is different, the team must embrace the belief that it can impact student success and the actions it observes can lead to promising initiatives on any campus. Use Figure 5.3 to brainstorm potential organizational observations.

As you prepare for these observations, remember that specificity is key. You are looking for clear evidence of implementation and success and specific actions the team has taken to achieve

FIGURE 5.3 Planning Your Observations

Data Point to Investigate From Your PLC	Potential Observation Source	Can This Observation Be Conducted Virtually?	What You Hope to See	How It Can Apply to Your Organization	When You Will Conduct the Observation to Make it Timely

them. Be sure to schedule time to debrief and ask follow-up questions. Before you leave the campus, you should have a strong sense of what your next steps will be. No initiative is perfect, but having a clear understanding of how a school made an impact on a focus area will help your team develop their own plan. Take your findings to the PLC and incorporate them into your PDSA cycle to accelerate their impact.

••

We must strive for continuous improvement in order to address the focus areas determined by the PLC, using every resource and strategy available to meet students' needs and creating new ones if needed.

••

Professional Development Linked to Formative Data Page

Now that you have your PLC in place and have planned out observations, you will need to share your findings with your organization to develop your own next steps. Will you adopt the observed initiative as you saw it? Did the observation inspire you to conduct further research on your own time? How will you clearly communicate the connection between your observations and the data points your team is focusing on?

Begin by showing how your takeaways inform the data points. The connection should be clear and direct to ensure that conversations focus on implementation and next steps instead of on the applicability of the takeaways. Ideally, your real-time formative data system will have space for you to link the next steps next to the data points they will address. If this is not logistically possible, make an online one-pager that links to both the data points and the findings. Include predictions for how the observation takeaways will impact the focus data points, and establish a timeline that aligns with your PDSA cycle.

Next, build your team's capacity for developing and leading professional development on implementing the action steps stemming from the data points, the observations, and the PLC conversations. Reflect on the support your organizational leaders will need to:

— Access the data.
— Analyze the data.
— Develop actionable next steps based on the data.
— Implement the actionable next steps.
— Assess their effectiveness.

To maximize the effectiveness of these professional development efforts, link the session content, resources, and screencasts directly to the formative data points and PDSA cycle discussions on one website or collaborative document. By eliminating the steps needed for participants to make the connections, you will greatly increase their useability, enhance participant buy-in, and reduce lost time in drawing conclusions. Having a one-stop destination for the data, the PLC work, and the professional development to address the data points is critical for moving quickly and maximizing the impact of your efforts. Use Figure 5.4 for your implementation plan.

Professional development does not need to be limited to traditional training sessions; it can be hands-on at school

FIGURE 5.4 One-Stop Destination Planning

What platform will you use for your one-stop destination (a website, a Google Doc, etc.)?	
Who will have access to the page?	
Who will be the primary manager?	
Can your real-time formative data system, your PLC documents, and your professional development resources all be linked to it?	
How will this page connect with your organizational vision?	

CONNECTION TO COMPANION BOOK

As you consider best practices to include in professional development, consider where best practices in the classroom will fit into the plan. Teachers can provide a vast collection of best practices learned from formative assessments, especially those developed and analyzed collaboratively; these should be included in the organization level formative data plan. Their experience and insight working directly with students will offer expertise that other data sources cannot replace. The companion book on formative data in the classroom provides more information on how to harness this information to impact student success.

sites, collaborating exploring implementation strategies and applying them, etc. Reflect on what supports your organizational members will need to apply the next steps developed by your PLC, and plan for the most direct approach for implementation.

Since you are aiming for change, use this opportunity to be as innovative as possible with your training and supports. Most importantly, you will need to reinforce the constantly iterative process of learning as leaders and promote continuous reflection and improvement. This is a critical element of the PDSA cycle and should not be downplayed. Vendlinski et al. (2008) explain, "The research literature and our experience suggest that scaffolding the assessment development process for teachers and providing a means whereby assessments can be continually 'polished' should improve the quality of classroom formative assessments" (p. 11). We must strive for continuous improvement in order to address the focus areas determined by the PLC, using every resource and strategy available to meet students' needs and creating new ones if needed.

Including a Wide Variety of Departments to Maximize Perspective and Expertise

Many of the challenges revealed by the data are complex and require carefully crafted action steps to address them. Often, they need input and action from multiple departments working cohesively as a team toward a common goal. Addressing gaps in learning, for example, may require professional development on differentiated instructional strategies from the teaching and learning department, access to instructional technology from the information and technology department, and socioemotional support from the student health and wellness department. Bringing together the expertise and perspective from multiple departments may take more time, but it ensures a more cohesive and comprehensive solution. Use technology to facilitate the conversations between departments and consolidate ideas to reach strategies and resources that maximize student success. Throughout the process, be sure to keep the focus on the data points to ensure that progress can be measured and that everyone involved understands the purpose for the action steps. As mentioned earlier in this chapter, look at specific students to see how each department can do its part in meeting their unique needs. McKay et al. (2020) states,

> In today's data-driven environment, decision-makers and the public seek information that is relevant, reliable, and complete as they assess the efficacy of policies and programs already in place and consider new policy options. Public agencies are often called upon to provide the needed information, even though on their own they may lack access to all the data required to paint a complete picture. (p. 1)

Bringing everyone together will ensure greater success.

FORMATIVE DATA FOR SOCIAL JUSTICE

As champions of formative assessment, we must ensure that every student's needs are met, regardless of their background, learning modality, or language proficiency. To do this, include experts from a variety of departments and insist on their hands-on involvement in formative data analysis. Leaders from the Special Education department, for example, can offer expertise for supporting students with learning disabilities that cannot be matched elsewhere; minimizing their role in the conversation can minimize the impact on the students they serve.

Key Takeaways

In this chapter, we explored how real-time formative data points can lead to action steps using professional learning communities that utilize a Plan-Do-Study-Act cycle. This regular data analysis and subsequent action process will maintain focus on desired objectives and track progress until they are met. Peer observations, in-person and virtual, can help the team better understand best practices and learn how to implement them on a large scale. Preparing your organization to use them requires professional development, which can come in a variety of formats depending on the focus area. Linking your real-time formative data system, PLC work, and professional development resources in one place increases efficiency and effectiveness, reducing lost time and maximizing cohesiveness. Throughout the process, including a wide variety of departments can help develop strategies and resources that meet the unique needs of each student. Use technology to facilitate cohesiveness and efficiency. Implementing this plan with fidelity sets the framework for a data-driven organizational culture that prioritizes all students' success. Over the past five chapters, we can see how this approach can bring us closer to an equity-focused vision; in the final chapter, we will examine how it can redefine your organization and prepare its members for the next level of student success.

6

Building a Data-Driven Culture of Innovation

Part I: The Need to Reevaluate How We Use Data in Our Organizations

Changing Data Considerations Due to . . . *(Introduction)*
♦ Advancements in Technology Changing Formative Data Use
♦ Loss of Consistent Summative Data From Previous Academic Years
♦ Concerns About Data Reliability Due to Limited Measures

NECESSITATE NEED TO REVISIT VISION

Your Organization's Vision and Beliefs *(Chapter 1)*
♦ Assessing Your Organization's Vision
♦ Reflecting on Your Beliefs About Student Learning and Your Role
♦ Where Formative Data Fits In

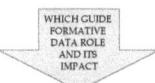
WHICH GUIDE FORMATIVE DATA ROLE AND ITS IMPACT

The Impact of Formative Data on Student Success *(Chapter 2)*
♦ Formative Data Fosters Educators' Growth Mindset
♦ Formative Data Informs Planning and Focus Areas
♦ Formative Data Facilitates Differentiation and Promotes Equity

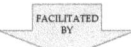
FACILITATED BY

Part II: Effective Formative Data Use for Leaders

Effective Formative Data Use to Drive Organizational Change *(Chapter 3)*	Using Instructional Technology to Effectively Address Formative Data *(Chapter 4)*	Analyzing Formative Data Collaboratively to Identify and Celebrate Best Practices *(Chapter 5)*
♦ How *Actionable* Is the Data You Are Gathering? ♦ How *Timely* Is the Data You Are Gathering? ♦ How Much Data Do You Need? ♦ How Much Time Will It Take to Collect the Data, and Will You Be Able to Address All the Data You Collect?	♦ Efficiently Gathering Formative Data ♦ Identifying and Addressing Validation Concerns to Ensure Broader Impact ♦ Implementing a Collaborative Plan-Do-Study-Act Cycle to Address Data	♦ PLCs using the PDSA cycle ♦ Peer Observations—In-Person and Virtual ♦ Professional Development Linked to Formative Data Page ♦ Including a Wide Variety of Departments to Maximize Perspective and Expertise

WHICH WILL LEAD TO

Building a Data-Driven Culture of Innovation *(Chapter 6)*
♦ **Re-envisioning Professional Development on Formative Data for All Educators**
♦ Reflecting on the Focus on Summative and Formative Data
♦ Fostering a Data-Driven Organizational Culture

> The COVID-19 pandemic dramatically shifted how we view formative data and how we incorporate technology in our work, and this pivotal moment serves as an unprecedented opportunity to transform our practice.

Re-envisioning Professional Development on Formative Data for All Educators

In the first five chapters, we journeyed through the process of establishing an equity-based organizational vision that utilized formative data to provide differentiated supports and resources to ensure student success. These efforts are not isolated steps; they are all part of a concerted effort to transform the culture of your organization and change the way we use technology to build student capacity. The COVID-19 pandemic dramatically shifted how we view formative data and how we incorporate technology in our work, and this pivotal moment serves as an unprecedented opportunity to transform our practice. The last chapter touched upon the need for professional development to connect formative data to actionable next steps; this final chapter will explore the development of an effective training program in greater detail in order to transform your organization's culture. It is important to note that "professional development" in this context includes any trainings, experiences, or opportunities designed to build the team's capacity for formative data analysis and planning next steps.

Let's begin by revisiting your organizational vision from Chapter 1. That vision served as the foundation for your real-time formative data system in Chapter 4 and your PLC-driven data analysis plan in Chapter 5. These critical elements, however, only serve as logistical steps if your team has not fully embraced the impact of formative data on decision-making. Simply sharing the importance of formative data will not convince everyone that the organization must consistently be data-driven; a data-driven organizational culture embeds formative data use in all facets of planning and action. This step involves actively modeling the new focus on formative data. Hattie (2012) explains

> that teachers and school leaders are responsible for cultural changes in schools; they do not change by mandate, but specific displacement of existing norms, structures, and processes by others—"the process of cultural change depends fundamentally on modeling the new values and behaviors that you expect to displace the existing ones' (Elmore, 2004, p. 11). (p. 150)

The first step in modeling the use of formative data as an essential element of planning and supports is to communicate it to everyone in the organization. Make your intentions clear but note that simply mandating formative data use will not have the desired effect; rather, your communication should be designed to give everyone context for the heightened focus on formative data. For maximum impact, the board should share this vision and expect formative data updates to be a regular part of each board meeting. The focus areas discussed in each meeting should include specific data points that the team will monitor and professional development around addressing them. Initial training for the entire organization will bring everyone together for a clear understanding of the heightened role formative data will play in decision-making and action. To reinforce this notion, include formative data in every leadership discussion, and consider these updates to those conversations:

- ♦ Avoid calling them general "meetings," which may not be associated with more traditional conversations about logistics. Collectively choose another title that better

describes your focus on student success and data-driven decision-making.
- Conclude each one with a timeline for action steps, including what the team will do and what updates it will bring. These next steps should be included in the agenda and linked directly to the PDSA cycle document the team is using. The more you streamline logistics, the more the team will make connections between team conversations, PLC work, and the PDSA cycle to increase cohesiveness.
- Focus on areas that you can measure progress on and incorporate into your PLC work. If a focus area cannot be measured, either quantitatively or qualitatively, how will you know if your efforts are impacting student success? If organizational leaders believe that a particular focus area warrants prioritization but it is difficult to measure, ask probing questions to dig deeper into the focus area until you find elements that can be measured. This step may take additional time, but being able to track progress and make adjustments will ultimately lead to faster results. Once again, "move slow to move fast."
- Consider how each department can contribute to the focus area and how each will measure their progress. Show how their work informs other departments as part of one collective effort. As with the second point, cohesiveness will lead to better results, both in practice and in stakeholder perception.

••
A data-driven organizational culture embeds formative data use in all facets of planning and action.
••

Once the importance of formative data is established as a critical part of your organization's vision, it will become easier to secure buy-in and funding for professional development specifically around data analysis. In addition to professional development on specific data analysis strategies, be sure to include trainings to facilitate a philosophical understanding of a data-driven cycle of inquiry and professional learning communities. The ideal professional development opportunity will include:

- A combination of theory and practice to help participants understand the philosophy behind the practice and have an opportunity to apply it.
- Modeling practices being shared during professional development so participants can see it in action and more readily apply it.
- Observations of leaders implementing the concepts shared during training sessions followed by opportunities for questions.

Including these elements to go beyond traditional professional development sessions can maximize the impact of your efforts. Hattie's research on the factors that impact student achievement confirms this. Based on his findings, Hattie (2009) explains, "The four types of instruction found to be most effective on teacher knowledge and behavior were: observation of actual classroom methods; microteaching; video/audio feedback; and practice" (p. 120). In other words, hands-on learning opportunities based on observed practices, feedback, and application yield the greatest results. These are critical for classroom instruction, but they can also be applied to learning at the organizational level.

All sessions should begin with the organizational vision and objectives that clearly align to it. You may begin by having participants engage in an activity to connect the objectives to the vision instead of simply sharing it. If you will use a slidedeck as part of your training, be sure to limit the number of slides and text and instead focus on interactive and exploratory activities to facilitate discussion and planning. When we developed the

FIGURE 6.1 Assessing Your Professional Development Needs

Potential Professional Development Need	How It Connects to Your Organizational Vision	Current Organizational Level of Competency	Stakeholder Groups Who Will Need This Training	Most Effective Format for the Training	Timeline: When Is This Training Needed?	How Will You Assess the Effectiveness of This Training?
Understanding the difference between formative and summative data.						
Using the Plan-Do-Study-Act cycle of inquiry to measure progress.						
Using the PLC model to guide data conversations.						
Understanding the organization's formative data access system.						
[Add other options here]						
[Add other options here]						
[Add other options here]						
[Add other options here]						

district's flagship professional growth series on blended learning, we limited each two-hour module to approximately ten slides of content in order to increase opportunities for collaboration, discussion, and content implementation. While there is no correct number of slides for each training, keep in mind that presentations with large numbers of slides will by design limit the amount of time participants have to apply their learning. Your organization's professional development needs will vary; use Figure 6.1 to determine which focus areas your organization will need additional support for and how you will provide it. In all cases, consider how each will further advance your organizational vision for real-time formative data.

Depending on your organization's experience and competency level with formative data use, these learning opportunities may need to be spread out over more than one year. Apply our takeaways on formative data to the professional development process by gathering information on initial needs as well as feedback from each opportunity. Use these formative data points to track learning progress and identify additional supports needed. You can also use formative data to assess the effectiveness of the professional development offerings. Consider gathering data on the percentage of the organization that has received formative data analysis training and the difference in outcomes between the efforts of those who have received different professional development opportunities.

•••

Professional development sessions taken in isolation won't transform your organizational culture, but a carefully planned program that builds on a consistent focus and connects to the organizational vision at every turn can do exactly that.

•••

To maximize the effectiveness of your professional development offerings, each successive opportunity should build on the prior session, and opportunities for application should be included between them. In our district, our blended learning training series includes applications between training modules to maximize learning. Participants earn technical certifications, lead professional development at their school sites based on the best practices they learned about, and conduct peer observations specifically focused on blended learning implementation. The system helps participants make sense of the training modules and see how they can directly impact instructional practice. These opportunities were designed from the beginning and included in the program timeline to ensure cohesiveness between the training modules and the applications. Plan ahead so that these connections are authentic and lead to deeper learning experiences for all involved. Professional development sessions taken in isolation won't transform your organizational culture, but a carefully planned program that builds on a consistent focus and connects to the organizational vision at every turn can do exactly that.

CONNECTION TO COMPANION BOOK

Be sure that teachers are key members of the professional development planning team as their experience with formative assessments and data will be critical. The companion book explores their role in gathering and analyzing formative data at the classroom level, and the data points they identify are essential parts of your organizational professional development program.

Reflecting on the Focus on Summative and Formative Data

A dramatic shift in organizational culture can also arise from honest conversations about real-time formative data compared to summative data. Most organizations focus heavily on summative data points for obvious reasons: they are the focus of accountability departments and become available to the public. The focus on summative data is not necessarily driven by educators' belief that it is critical for student learning. The nature of summative assessments also impacts student perceptions about the role of data in learning. Researchers Haimovitz and Dweck state,

> Children today are growing up in a world where performance on high stakes tests is often treated as a more important goal than deeper learning. Research shows that many students may see such tests as measures of not just their current skills and knowledge but also of their intelligence and, in fact, their lifelong intelligence. (p. 1856)

This is not to say that summative data does not play an important role in measuring growth over time at critical points; it just needs to be joined by formative data points to inform learning for both educators and students. Often, summative assessments offer data on a timeline that isn't conducive to real-time actionable next steps and provides more data than could be acted upon. For these reasons, summative data is not the most effective type of information for differentiating instruction and supports in real-time to serve diverse learners. Equitably serving all students requires a personalized approach to instruction, and that can best be served by effectively gathering and acting on formative data. Therefore, an organizational vision that prioritizes equity must also prioritize formative data analysis.

The good news is that focusing on formative data will inevitably lead to strong summative data. In fact, the more consistently we gather and act on formative data, the more we will see the positive impact on our summative results. Gathering and acting on real-time formative data as much as possible accelerates this impact considerably. Note that gathering formative data alone does not lead to this impact: it is the action we take on the formative data using our PDSA cycle of inquiry and the collaborations in our PLCs that makes a difference. So how can you persuade your team to adopt an organizational culture that prioritizes formative data despite the powerful influences of accountability and publicity that comes with summative data?

••

The more consistently we gather and act on formative data, the more we will see the positive impact on our summative results. Gathering and acting on real-time formative data as much as possible accelerates this impact considerably.

••

Start by showing the team examples of improvement over time in scenarios outside of education. Imagine for a moment that you decide to run in next year's marathon. How successful would you be if you ran for a couple of hours each day and then showed up on the day of the marathon hoping you are ready to complete the race? How confident would you feel that you will be successful? Now consider an alternate approach in which you run each day, compare your distance each time, gather data on how you feel, and make adjustments to your diet, stretching regimen, and water intake. As race day approaches, you know how close you are each day to being ready to complete all 26.2 miles. By the time you reach the night before the marathon, you have a clear sense of whether you will be successful or not because you have a body of evidence that shows how successful you have been and what factors facilitated that success. By the time you reach the summative assessment, you already know how it is going to go. You can use a wide variety of examples to convey this message; anything that requires a consistent build over time can be used.

As a high school mathematics teacher, I used a similar approach for utilizing formative and summative assessments. To start, I used multiple formative assessments throughout each lesson to determine progress and identify needs for differentiated support. I used questions with clickers built into direct instruction and individualized whiteboards for students to show their learning among other strategies to identify student mastery levels. Lessons would typically end with an "exit ticket," a brief assessment at the end of the class designed to assess students' overall mastery levels for the lesson; data from this assessment would then inform individualized office hour supports for students that afternoon to ensure students received the support they need to be successful before they left campus that day. If the formative data I collected throughout the lesson indicated that the lesson as a whole was not successful, I would skip the exit ticket at the end because I already had enough data to reveal student mastery levels; there was no need to use instructional time for it when the outcome was already clear. Instead, I would ask other questions to better understand how the lesson could be improved. Were there prerequisite concepts or skills that necessitate additional review? Do stronger connections between the concepts in this lesson need to be made to ones previously explored? The more thoughtful your formative assessments are throughout the lesson, the more clearly you will know which direction you'll need to go next. Every prompt you offer should return a wealth of information to you to maximize its impact. For example, if you use a multiple-choice question to gather formative data, each incorrect answer choice should reveal something about student understanding. If the correct answer is 3, your incorrect answer choices should not be 2, 4, 5, and 6. Students who choose one of the incorrect answers in this scenario do not share any information with you other than they did not answer correctly. Instead, devise incorrect answers that reveal student misconceptions so you get more information on next steps. This way, you get information from the formative assessment even if students answer incorrectly. Of course, this requires more planning time, but you will easily make up that time because your response to the formative assessment will be much more targeted and, therefore, more effective.

•••

By the time you reach the summative assessment, you already know how it is going to go.

•••

Think about how you get buy-in from your team on shifting the priority on summative data to formative data, especially considering most organizations' extensive history of spotlighting summative data. The accountability reports and public availability of summative data will continue to drive the efforts of many team members for understandable reasons; we cannot ignore the fact that summative data can have a dramatic impact on recognition and enrollment, funding, and other factors critical to the community. I am not advocating for disregarding summative data or downplaying its importance; rather, I am suggesting that focusing actionable next steps on formative data points will ultimately have a greater impact on summative data. To make this connection, your team must believe that their efforts in formative data analysis and next steps using a cycle of inquiry will directly impact the summative data points. If there is a disconnect between the work around formative data and summative data outcomes, then there will be little incentive to prioritize formative data over summative data.

Stakeholder community members such as parents, guardians, and students will also need to understand this shift in focus from summative data to formative data. Communication with these groups is particularly critical because many have traditionally only had access to summative data reports available publicly online. They often do not have access to formative data points and may be unfamiliar with the philosophy and action behind them. Your messaging to them is a critical step in transforming your organizational focus to formative data. For administrators, teachers, and other educators, training must be provided to convey the philosophy on formative data use as well as how to maximize its impact using a

Plan-Do-Study-Act cycle of inquiry in professional learning communities. This work will naturally flow into other topics, such as grading practices and opportunities for students to self-monitor. For parents and guardians, the messaging should include information about how enhanced formative data use

FIGURE 6.2 Planning Formative Data Messaging

	Team members (teachers, administrators, etc.)	Parents/ Guardians	Students
How have you shared your new organizational vision with each group?			
How does your organization currently communicate summative data to each group?			
How familiar is each group with real-time formative data? How do you know?			
For each group, how will you communicate the connection between summative data and formative data?			
What training opportunities will you offer each group (professional development, stakeholder meetings, etc.)? What is the justification for any difference in approach between groups?			
What data will you gather to determine the effectiveness of your communication and training plan?			

positively impacts students' growth mindset and their ability to grow as independent learners. These are critical for future success long after students graduate. The same messaging can be shared with students, though adding opportunities for students to self-monitor their learning using formative data will dramatically improve their development as independent learners. Use Figure 6.2 to plan your messaging to your team and to your stakeholder community.

Questions may arise as to why this shift in focus to formative data is happening now. If formative data points have been a critical part of determining next steps for students for years, why are we beginning to prioritize them now with our vision and our organizational goals? A strong justification for this shift lies in the greatly improved access to and expertise in technology over recent years, which translates to better access to real-time formative data and more efficient processes for analyzing and acting on formative data. As we explored in previous chapters, formative data access must be simplified so that our limited time and energy can be largely spent on analysis and next steps; with recent advances in technology, we can do exactly that.

To stay true to this message, consider collaboratively working on an organizational expectation to communicate student progress with real-time data on a regular basis. Ideally, students will receive training on how to self-monitor and be aware of their progress so they can share information about their strengths and areas of focus with their families. Building students' capacity to do this can be done through consistent opportunities to self-monitor and receive feedback. For example, any rubric used can include a self-assessment section in which students self-rate themselves and offer justifications for their rating. These can be compared to the feedback provided by the instructor to calibrate expectations and better understand next steps. An online portal through which students can monitor their strengths and areas of growth can also be helpful, especially when combined with an organizational philosophy that offers students multiple opportunities to demonstrate mastery.

Students can continuously strive for mastery in previously missed areas, building their strengths as well as their growth mindset. These efforts will undoubtedly be met with some skepticism as they can be striking departures from normal practices, but any innovative practice that challenges traditional thinking typically does. If you are confident that your efforts are putting students' interests front and center and will maximize student success, you will find the justification needed to keep pushing forward.

I am not advocating for disregarding summative data or downplaying its importance; rather, I am suggesting that focusing actionable next steps on formative data points will ultimately have a greater impact on summative data.

IMPLEMENTATION TIP

Keep in mind that summative data points become available at the end to show overall progress, but formative data points are the ones that will inform actionable next steps. For this reason, consider ways to increase formative data prioritization over summative data in your organization. Summative data points are often considered "high stakes" and therefore capture attention more readily, but they are not as helpful as formative data in guiding the direction of your organization. Summative data points will take care of themselves if you focus instead on formative data points.

Fostering a Data-Driven Organizational Culture

In your efforts to shift your organizational culture to one driven by real-time formative data, keep in mind that not everyone will immediately buy-in, and that is okay. Hattie (2009) cites research that suggests initially only a few teachers (typically those open to change, more educated, who have a greater store of knowledge, are self-confident, and are not so concerned with norms than others) begin trying innovation. Then when there is sufficient critical mix, many more begin to innovate, but it is hard to get acceptance from the final 20 percent plus. Teachers will not just move from not doing a new behavior to doing it; they go through decision phases. (p. 257)

If we wait for all team members of the organization to buy-in to this innovative approach to decision-making, we may never reach the opportunity to launch the initiative. We must proceed with an initial group and continuously generate interest and adoption from others, which can be accelerated if we showcase the benefits of the approach regularly and reinforce the notion that as educators, we must embrace a growth mindset and continuously strive for improvement. There must be a sense of urgency around our work because students—especially at-risk students who need differentiated supports—do not have the luxury of waiting for us to onboard everyone before we move forward.

Reflect on your team's readiness to embrace this new organizational culture focused on formative data. Consider how they will react and how eager they will be to communicate it to the stakeholder community. Use Figure 6.3 to plan your next steps for each of the three potential team member groups. Keep in mind that while they may be in different initial phases of buy-in when you start, you must continue to work with all three groups to build their capacity and increase their investment in your organizational culture. On an organizational level, your efforts will only go as far as your effectiveness in soliciting buy-in and engagement.

Do not be discouraged if your initial reflection reveals a limited buy-in from key members; it is always possible to expand. Your goal is to ultimately offer equitable supports for all

FIGURE 6.3 Next Steps for Buy-In

	Team members who will initially buy-in	Team members who will need time	Team members who will likely stay reluctant
Identify the key members of each group.			
Identify critical members of your team who can help develop a communication plan.			
Describe how you will approach the key members of each group.			
Explain how you will engage them in sharing messaging.			
Describe how you will measure the effectiveness of your approach.			
Identify your expected timeline for reaching a critical mass of team members that will advocate for the new organizational vision.			

students through data-driven differentiation, and keeping the students in mind when you share the vision will be critical in gathering buy-in. Data analysis is a critical step in the process, but do not forget that there are students behind the numbers.

Include specific students who may benefit, as described in Chapter 5, and humanize this effort. You may even consider identifying a few students who experienced success from differentiated supports based on a teacher's formative data use and ask if they would be willing to share their story. Remember that your audience, like you, decided to become educators to help students succeed. This shift in organizational vision aims to fulfill that goal using our newfound expertise with technology; it is no different than the intention we started with when we first became teachers.

TECH TIP

In the spirit of transparency and fostering an organizational culture built on continuous growth, give broad access to the formative data platform to stakeholders who can benefit and improve their practice. Include the links to best practices, and be sure to limit access to personal identifying information.

Success Celebration Events With Best Practice Sharing

Professionals sometimes fear data because it may expose shortcomings in their practice. An evaluation, test, or feedback meeting all have the potential of highlighting areas of growth. While we know our work is not flawless, we shy away from making it known to others. It is human nature: no one wants their failures to be publicized. Even worse, we may be compared to others who are performing at a higher level. For educators, this is magnified by the fact that anything other than perfection suggests that we are letting some students fail since there are students behind the data points. For deeply committed teachers, administrators, and district leaders, this can be a painful reality. It also makes the idea of introducing a data-driven organizational culture a tougher sell. For some, it may be more comfortable to limit conversations about data until they are unavoidable, such as at the end of the year when states release summative data. How then do we pitch a proposal that may generate anxiety and initiate unproductive comparisons between educators and students in different classrooms?

Like most initiatives, the success of the proposal comes down to framing. Examining formative data points can be used to focus on gaps in student learning, or it can be a way to achieve our initial goal to maximize student learning. By focusing on a cycle of inquiry that monitors data and action steps to show progress over time, we can identify how our efforts are bringing us closer to our goal. This latter approach is student-centered and celebrates student success. Focus on progress, not only outcomes. Every school, student, or department starts from a different baseline, and prioritizing outcomes lessens the evaluative nature of data analysis and fosters growth mindset. No matter where we begin, we can always learn and grow. Fostering growth mindset means anything other than perfection is not failure; we just continue pushing so all students can be successful.

Take celebrating success to a new level by making it an official part of your formative data program. As you monitor progress in the PLCs, carefully document the actionable steps that the team takes to impact the outcome. When notable gains result, celebrate them publicly. Successes can be shared with school sites at board meetings, open house events, and principals' meetings. They can also be used to inform the practice of others in the organization if opportunities to share are built into your program. Consider establishing a "data festival" in which schools share an area of focus, what they did to address it, and the data points that show the impact of those efforts. Teachers and school leaders can visit different booths at the festival to learn about the actions and how they can be applied in their schools. You can enhance the experience by:

- *Encouraging innovative approaches to sharing each school's plan*: High-quality videos built in collaboration with students, websites documenting the challenges faced and how the school overcame them, and interactive graphs can all bring the plans to life and engage others. As much as possible, involve students in the process. They are the reason for this work, and including them reminds participants that they are behind the data. This is also a great opportunity to build students' capacity for understanding their own progress and getting one step closer to becoming independent learners.
- *Creating an easy-to-follow series of steps that can help another school get started with implementation*: Whether on a one-pager or an online document with hyperlinks built in, paving the way for others to replicate success can accelerate implementation and lead to quicker results. Of course, no two schools will implement a plan exactly the same way, but having a general guide to get started will be of great help.
- *Including students in the planning and implementation of the festival*: Students should play an integral part, including sharing their successes, playing music, and contributing artwork. These efforts can bring the festival to life and reinforce the celebratory nature of the event.

A formative data festival can also serve as a way to bring the organization together. We sometimes hear that different schools or departments "work in silos" because of limited opportunities to interact, share, and learn from each other. How often do principals have an opportunity to collaborate with their counterparts in other schools? How often can teachers observe teachers in other schools? This is a great opportunity to connect with others and truly become a *unified* school district as we work toward a common goal of ensuring *all* students' success. An event like this can magnify the impact of formative data points

> **FORMATIVE DATA FOR SOCIAL JUSTICE**
>
> Be sure to emphasize and celebrate initiatives that promote equity. Resources, initiatives, and supports that schools used to close the achievement gap and facilitate equity and access should be highlighted as they foster an organizational culture and vision that is dedicated to ensuring all students succeed.

by creating a space for several schools and departments to learn from them and apply their takeaways to other students.

Focus on progress, not only outcomes. Every school, student, or department starts from a different baseline, and prioritizing outcomes lessens the evaluative nature of data analysis and fosters growth mindset. No matter where we begin, we can always learn and grow. Fostering growth mindset means anything other than perfection is not failure; we just continue pushing so all students can be successful.

> **TECH TIP**
>
> As you celebrate initiatives that led to gains in a variety of areas, consider using a system that allows participants to nominate each for awards. Examples include awards for most innovative, greatest impact on equity, and most replicable. A simple tool such as Google Forms can be used by participants to submit their nominations as it can be used on mobile devices.

Key Takeaways

In this final chapter, we examined how your new organizational vision can help re-envision what professional development on real-time formative data can look like, facilitate reflection on the critical differences between summative and formative data, and foster a data-driven culture that celebrates successes. Each of these takes a great deal of time and effort to incorporate with fidelity throughout the organization, and rushing through the process can lead to superficial investment from stakeholders, which can ultimately result in short-lived implementation and abandonment when challenges arise. Shifting an organization toward a vision that differs significantly from standard practice is not easy, but the benefits of differentiated supports based on formative data are well worth the effort. Persevere and see your plan through—the impact on student success will become immediately evident.

Conclusion

Through our journey in this book, we steadily moved toward developing an organizational culture steeped in real-time formative data access and analysis. Part I of this book focused on understanding the importance of formative data points at the organizational level and exploring how we might maximize their impact through real-time access thanks to technology. We examined the need to reevaluate how we approach data analysis based on advancements in technology, the loss of consistent summative data from previous academic years, and concerns about data reliability due to limited measures. These factors drove us to find more impactful ways to utilize data, particularly in real-time to maximize student achievement. We could not act on a systemwide scale, however, until we established a clear organizational vision for data analysis.

Before defining a formative data-driven vision, we examined your current organizational vision and how applicable it is to the students in your schools. We reflected on your organization's beliefs about student learning and your role as an educator and created a revised vision that put formative data front and center. To make the vision meaningful for all stakeholders, we investigated its impact on fostering educators' growth mindset, informing planning and focus, and facilitating differentiation to promote equity.

In Part II, we developed a plan to bring this vision to life by getting into the details of how to identify critical data points, efficiently collect them, and use best practices to equitably address them. We started by learning how to identify formative data points that can lead to action, determine the level of detail that may be needed, choose the most effective timeline for analysis, and consider the complexity involved in gathering the data. With these pieces in place, we set the groundwork for the development of a real-time formative data system to efficiently analyze data that can have a direct impact on student achievement.

Next, we reviewed how to plan your team's approach for effectively using technology to gather and analyze formative data. We examined how the PDSA cycle can lead to action steps using professional learning communities. This regular data analysis and subsequent action process will maintain focus on desired objectives and track progress until they are met. We saw how linking your formative data system, PLC work, and professional development resources in one place can increase efficiency and effectiveness. Finally, we examined how your new organizational vision can help re-envision what professional development on formative data can look like, facilitate reflection on the critical differences between summative and formative data, and foster a data-driven culture that celebrates successes.

Establishing a real-time data-driven culture using these steps will undoubtedly have a dramatic impact on students, particularly at-risk students who will receive the timely and personalized supports they need to be successful. Absenteeism, socioemotional well-being, behavior, progress toward graduation, and other critical elements of success in K-12 can all be impacted. These factors, of course, must be addressed at the same time as effective classroom instruction that prioritizes differentiation based on formative assessments. A deeper exploration on formative data use in the classroom can be found in this book's companion, *Harnessing Formative Data for K-12 Teachers*. That book addresses many of the concepts addressed in this book but focuses on them at the classroom level.

Think back to the cross-country road trip described back in the second chapter. In that analogy, the lead car was responsible for providing differentiated supports to make sure all cars make it to the end of the journey. That one lead car needed to carry extra tires of different sizes, lots of gas canisters, and a host of tools and resources to address any challenge. Now picture if an entire organization—working in close collaboration and with one vision—is committed to helping the cars make it to the finish line. The caravan can include tow trucks, a van filled with tires, and vehicles following the group, all of which are in constant communication and checking on student cars regularly. Not only are they providing differentiated supports as needed, but also they are beginning to identify parts of the journey that seem to require additional assistance each time and preparing help in advance. This level of collaboration and commitment only comes if everyone in the group is invested in a common outcome driven by a common vision. A group of students making this journey will be in good hands and highly likely to reach their destination. Investing the time and effort to build an organizational culture driven by data will lead to this type of collective efficacy. Imagine a school system in which all supports are driven by student needs and stakeholders collaboratively work toward addressing them through an iterative process that consistently monitors progress. Combining the organizational level best practices discussed in this book with the classroom strategies on formative data in the companion book will transform the educational experience of students and prepare them as lifelong independent learners.

References

Anderson, S., Leithwood, K. & Strauss, T. (2010). Leading Data Use in Schools: Organizational Conditions and Practices at the School and District Levels. *Leadership and Policy in Schools*, 9(3), 292–327.

Chung, G., Shel, T. & Kaiser, W. (2006). An Exploratory Study of a Novel Online Formative Assessment and Instructional Tool to Promote Students' Circuit Problem Solving. *The Journal of Technology, Learning, and Assessment*, 5(6), 1–27.

Dalby, D. & Swan, M. (2019). Using Digital Technology to Enhance Formative Assessment in Mathematics Classrooms. *British Journal of Educational Technology*, 50(2), 832–845.

DuFour, R. (2004, May 1). *What Is a "Professional Learning Community"?* Association for Supervision and Curriculum Development (ASCD). www.ascd.org/el/articles/what-is-a-professional-learning-community.

Dweck, C. (2007). Boosting Achievement with Messages That Motivate. *Education Canada*, 47(2), 6–10.

Dweck, C. (2010). Even Geniuses Work Hard. *Educational Leadership*, 68(1), 16–20.

Fatout, B. (2015). Inspiring Teacher Leadership Through Intentional Communication. *The National Center on Scaling Up Effective Schools*, 1–14.

Garcia-Lopez, A. & Garcia-Marazio, F. (2016). The Use of Technology in a Model of Formative Assessment. *Journal of Technology and Science Education*, 6(2), 91–103.

Haimovitz, K. & Dweck, C. (2017). The Origins of Children's Growth and Fixed Mindsets: New Research and a New Proposal. *Child Development*, 88(6), 1849–1859.

Hattie, J. (2009). *Visible Learning: A Synthesis of over 800 Meta-Analysis Relating to Achievement*. Routledge. 9780415528443

Hattie, J. (2012). *Visible Learning for Teachers: Maximizing Impact on Learning*. Routledge. 9780415528340.

Hord, S. M. (1997). Professional Learning Communities: Communities of Continuous Inquiry and Improvement. Southwest Educational Development Laboratory (contract no. RJ96006801). Office of Educational Research and Improvement, U.S. Department of Education.

Jeong, J., Gonzalez-Gomez, D. & Yllana Prieto, F. (2020). Sustainable and Flipped STEM Education: Formative Assessment Online Interface for Observing Pre-Service Teachers' Performance and Motivation. *Educational Sciences*, 10(283), 1–14.

Jorno, R. & Gynther, K. (2018). What Constitutes an "Actionable Insight" in Learning Analytics? *Journal of Learning Analytics*, 5(3), 198–221.

Luckin, R., Clark, W., Avramides, K., Hunter, J. & Martin, O. (2017). Using Teacher Inquiry to Support Technology-enhanced Formative Assessment: A Review of the Literature to Inform a New Method. *Interactive Learning Environments*, 25(1), 85–97.

MacLeod, K., Swart, W. & Paul, R. (2019). Continual Improvement of Online and Blended Teaching Using Relative Proximity Theory. *Decision Sciences Journal of Innovative Education*, 17(1), 53–75.

McKay, H., Haviland, S. & Michael, S. (2020). Building Trust for Inter-Organizational Data Sharing: The Case of the MLDE. *Western Interstate Commission for Higher Education*, 1–3.

Moen, R. & Norman, C. (2010). Circling Back: Clearing Up Myths About the Deming Cycle and Seeing How It Keeps Evolving. *Quality Progress*, 43(11), 22–28.

Nicholson, J., Capitelli, S., Richert, A., Wilson, C. & Bove, C. (2017). Teacher Leaders Building Foundations for Data-Informed Teacher Learning in One Urban Elementary School. *The New Educator*, 13(2), 170–189.

Nyland, R. (2018). A Review of Tools and Techniques for Data-Enabled Formative Assessment. *Journal of Educational Technology Systems*, 46(4), 505–526.

Piety, P. (2019). Components, Infrastructures, and Capacity: The Quest for the Impact of Actionable Data Use on P–20 Educator Practice. *Review of Research in Education*, 43(1). 394–421.

Rowland, C., Feygin, A., Lee, F., Gomez, S. & Rasmussen, C. (2018). Improving the Use of Information to Support Teaching and

Learning Through Continuous Improvement Cycles. *American Institutes for Research*, 1–64.

Schildkamp, K. (2019). Data-based Decision-making for School Improvement: Research Insights and Gaps. *Educational Research*, 61(3), 257–273.

Sears, R., Hopf, F., Torres-Ayala, A., Williams, C. & Skryzpek, L. (2019). Using Plan-Do-Study-Act Cycles and Interdisciplinary Conversations to Transform Introductory Mathematics Courses. *Problems, Resources, and Issues in Mathematics Undergraduate Studies (PRIMUS)*, 29(8), 881–902.

Sun, J., Przybylski, R. & Johnson, B. (2016). A Review of Research on Teachers' Use of Student Data: From the Perspective of School Leadership. *Educational Assessment, Evaluation and Accountability*, 28, 5–33.

Shirley, M. & Irving, K. (2014). Connected Classroom Technology Facilitates Multiple Components of Formative Assessment Practice. *Journal of Science Education and Technology*, 24, 56–58.

Streifer, P. & Schumann, J. (2005). Using Data Mining to Identify Actionable Information: Breaking New Ground in Data-Driven Decision Making. *Journal of Education for Students Placed at Risk*, 10(3), 281–293.

Uribe, S. & Vaughan, M. (2017). Facilitating Student Learning in Distance Education: A Case Study on the Development and Implementation of a Multifaceted Feedback System. *Distance Education*, 38(3), 288–301.

Vendlinski, T., Niemi, D. & Wang, J. (2008). Improving Formative Assessment Practice with Educational Information Technology. *National Center for Research on Evaluation, Standards, and Student Testing (CRESST)*, 1–17.

Wilkerson, S., Klute, M., Peery, B. & Liu, J. (2021). How Nebraska Teachers Use and Perceive Summative, Interim, and Formative Data. *National Center for Education Evaluation and Regional Assistance at the Institute of Educational Sciences (IES)*, 1–54.

Index

Note: Page numbers in *italics* indicate figures.

accountability: focus 52; reports 109; results, strengthening 53; systems, examination 12–13
achievement: gap, closure 10; improvement 49
actionability, consistency (importance) 51
actionable data: identification, data points (usage) 8–10; points, prioritization 52
actionable feedback 55
actionable formative data: accessibility/use, impact 5–6; experience 54–55
actionable next steps: development/implementation 91; focus 11; providing 10
actionable, term (indication) 47
actionable timeline 56
action steps: purpose, understanding 94; timelines 85, 101
active student-teacher collaboration, involvement 34
assessment: continuity 53; development process 93; primary function 34; systems, examination 12–13; technology support 6
at-risk students 9

backtracking, reduction 40
best practices: basis 105; consideration 93; identification/celebration, formative data analysis (usage) 81; sharing 115–118
boardrooms, message (sharing) 19
brainstorming *41*, 90
budget timelines 56
buy-in 22, 88–89, 112; establishment *89*; generation 35; increase 56; limited buy-in, revealing 113–115; steps *114*

California Assessment of Student Performance and Progress (CAASPP) 57
California School Dashboard 47, 54; metrics 64
Career Technical Education (CTE) 48
change: avoidance, issue 17; impact, power 35–36
circular reasoning, impact 17
classroom: cameras, usage 88; formative data points, usages 55; implementation 55; instruction 87; messages, sharing 19; teacher vision, establishment 19
cohesiveness (increase), PDSA cycle (usage) 101
collaboration: culture 84; opportunities, increase 104
collective creativity 83
content implementation 104
continual improvement system 73
continuous feedback loops, requirement 83
continuous improvement, approach 91
COVID-19 pandemic, impact 10–12, 99
cultural change, process (factors) 100
current year formative data, usage (importance) 11
customization functionality 50

data: access 67–70, 75, 92; accessibility, ease 67–70; action, timing (determination) 56; amount, requirement 57–58; demographic information, inclusion 42; festival, establishment 116; "just in time" examination 38; loss 67; metric, usage 64; monitoring 116; professional development planning team experience 105; reliability, concerns 12–13; reports, providing 67; saturation, drawback 48; symbolic data use/misuse/abuse 52; syncing requirements 64; systematization 64–67; teacher perceptions/attitudes 34; tracking 25; visualization system, usage 66
data, addressing 70; PDSA cycle, usage 72–77
data analysis 77, 92; conversations 85–86; disinterest/apprehension 34; frequency, determination 47; sessions, leading 24; steps 83; training 104
data collection: actionability, determination 47–53; opportunities (creation), instructional technology (usage) 6–8; time, amount (requirement) 56–59; timeliness, determination 53–55
data-driven culture, building 100
data-driven cycle of inquiry, philosophical understanding 102
data-driven decision making 84; role 19
data-driven environment 94
data-driven next steps, determination 24
data-driven organizational culture: formative data, embedding 100; fostering 112–115; impact 101; introduction 115–116
data-driven organization, vision (core) 39
data points: absence 71; addressing, urgency 75; analysis 59; collection, topic areas (list) 58; continuity (disruption), events change (impact) 12; continuity (disruption), metrics change (impact) 11; exploration 58, 59; factors 54; filtration 8; housing 8; identification 47; reduction 49; timeliness 12; unavailability 11; usage 8–10,72; usefulness 12, 42
data review 21; process 23
data-rich climate, challenge 57
data, usage 37, 52; importance 21; opportunities (creation), instructional technology (usage) 6–8; school leader responsibility 21
decision-making process, approach 21
demographic data: inclusion 69
demographic data, columns (addition) 51
demographic information, inclusion 42
diagnostic assessments, completion 56
diagnostic feedback, providing 53
differentiated instructional strategies 94
differentiated supports, providing 40
differentiated training, offering 54
differentiation: facilitation, formative data (impact) 39–42
differentiation, usage 20
digital technology, usage 51–52
distance learning experience 88

educational data/assessment program, usage 66
educators: formative data, professional development (re-envisioning) 99–105; growth mindset, formative data (usage) 31–37; internalization 36
English language proficiency 69
English Learners 50; progress 47
equity: ensuring 47; marker, impact 40; vision, reaching 81

equity promotion 118; formative data, facilitation 39–42
evidence-information conversations (facilitation), school administrator responsibility 31

feedback 50; actionable feedback 55; continuous feedback loops, requirement 83; diagnostic feedback, providing 53; generation 34; giving 31; importance 53
focus areas: formative data, impact 37–39
formative assessment: data 26; explanation 59; professional development planning team experience 105; usage 107
formative data 93; action 106; actionable next steps, providing 10; addressing, instructional technology (usage) 63; benefits 6–7; brainstorming 41; current year formative data, usage (importance) 11; dashboard, California School Dashboard model 11; data-driven organizational culture, impact 101; embedding 100; facilitation 39–42; financial services department usage 22; fit 24–26; focus, reflection 105–112; focus, shift 111; housing, dashboard (usage) 65; impact 31, 34–39; importance 101; messaging, planning *110*; organizational level 38; page, professional development (link) 91–93; perspective 84–85; prioritization 19, 112; professional development, re-envisioning 99–105; review, data reports (usage) 67; source 72; student health/wellness department usage 22; supports 85; timing, consideration 56; visual presentations, usage 39
formative data analysis 81; hands-on involvement 95; importance 42; organization plan, future-proof design 11; PDSA cycle, importance 73–74

formative data collection: consistency 107; demographic information, inclusion 42; efficiency 63–70; organization plan, future-proof design 11; sources 8
formative data-driven vision, defining 121
formative data platform: access 115; design 52
formative data points: access 63; collection 48; focus area determination 39; growth mindset, relationship 32, 33; identification 39; management system, creation 47
formative data system 38; building 51; development, steps *59*; impact 51–52
formative data use *23*, 101; change, technology advancements (impact) 32; effectiveness 47; process 25
formative evaluation, providing 37
formative system, customization 50

graduation rates 47; formative data points 54
growth mindset 31–37; cardinal rule 18–19; connection *33*; culture, development 31; focus 32; formative data points, connection 33; fostering 118; impact 110–111; long-term growth mindset 37; organization-wide growth mindset, reinforcement 18–19; prioritization 32; teacher reinforcement 32

high-level progress, assessment 25
hyperlinks, usage 77, 117

improvement actions, translation 52
innovation 53; culture 84; data-driven culture, building 99; networks 7; organizational focus 7; trying 113
in-person peer observations 87–91
inquiry cycle 82–83; data-driven cycle, philosophical understanding

102; management system, creation 47
inquiry cycle, determination 47
instruction: formative data, impact 26; personalized approach, requirement 106; problems, impact (maximization) 48–49; time, minimization 74
instructional adjustments, impact 32
instructional decision making 32
instructional practice strategies 54
instructional program, growth mindset element 32
instructional technology: data collection usage opportunities, creation 6–8; formative data, addressing 63
intervention, basis 85

language: English language proficiency 69; inclusion 20; proficiency (data) 20, 42, 95
leadership team: commitment 81; role, importance 37
leaders, observations 102
learning: acceleration, actionable formative data accessibility/use (impact) 5; culture, creation 35; depth 105; disabilities 20; educator belief 36; importance 18; improvement 53; loss 5; modalities 20, 95
logistical planning 26
long-term growth mindset 37

mastery, demonstration 111–112
meetings: general meetings, naming (avoidance) 100–101; scheduling 55; setting 73
metrics: change, impact 11; score 47
misconceptions (addressing), formative data points (usage) 55
modeling data, principal use 21
monitoring, technology support 6

observation plan *89–90*
observation, planning *90*

offline program, usage 67
one-stop destination planning 92
online document, development 24–25
on-the-fly formative assessments, usage 74
organization: beliefs 17, *23*; change, formative data use (impact) 47; graduation rate 56; system development 52
organizational culture: adoption 106–107; creation 22–23; transformation, absence 104; transparency/fostering 115
organizational growth process 37
organizational-level formative data points, continuation 40–41
organizational peer observation, buy-in (establishment) *89*
organizational vision 17, *26*; assessment 17–20; connection 104; development 25; examination 121–122; example *19*; focus 20; fulfillment 86; impact 32; member buy-in, requirement 22; reflection 20; requirement 85; shift, impact 18; updates 17
organization-wide growth mindset, reinforcement 18
outcomes: focus/prioritization 118; improvement 75; prioritization 116

peer observations 87–91; buy-in 88; logistical planning, usage 88
performance levels, cutoffs (shift) 11
Plan-Do-Study-Act (PDSA) cycle 37, 57, *73*; actions, implementation 75; cycle of inquiry 81; impact, examination 122; implementation 72–77; importance 73–74; power 86; usage 82–87, 101, 109–110
planned formative assessments, usage 74
planned professional development sessions 56
planning areas, formative data (impact) 37–39
platform: design 52; usage 8

post-pandemic leadership teams, learning loss 5
principals: leadership role 37; modeling data use 21
professional development (PD): attention/opportunities 21; effectiveness, maximization 92, 104; formative data page, link 91–93; importance 100; inclusion 93; limitation, absence 92–93; needs, assessment *103*; opportunity 102, 104; planned professional development sessions 56; planning team, experience 105; re-envisioning 99–105; requirement 32; sessions 88, 104, 105; windows, limitation 63
Professional Learning Communities (PLCs): data analysis conversations 85–86; elements 84; framework *87*; PDSA cycle, usage 82–87; placement 91; progress, monitoring 116; vision/goals 84; work 101
professional learning, principals (support) 34
progress: assessment, inquiry cycle (determination) 47; data-driven reflections, absence 21; focus 118; measurement, data points (usage) 72

real-time access 121
real-time data: analysis 25; usage 26, 64, 65
real-time formative data: collection/acting 107; conversation 33; impact 7; inclusion 20; points, analysis 86; student services department usage 22; summative data, comparison 105–106; teacher usage 22
real-time formative data system: building, considerations *38*; effectiveness 82; equity commitment 82
real-time quantitative data, usage 57–58
reflection questions, usage 54

resources: absence 36; engagement, creation 68; spending 18; usage 52
results, focus (importance) 86

school leaders: data use responsibility 21; goal-setting process stakeholders 48; policy translation 48
screencasts: usefulness 68; visual presentations, usage 39
self-monitoring, process 111
shared leadership 83
shared personal practice 83
shared values/vision 83
social justice: championing 71; emphasis 20
socioeconomic status (data) 42
spreadsheet export, usage 65
stakeholder community: communication 113; members, understanding 109–111
stakeholders 57–58; goal-setting process 48
standards-based questions, library (selection) 67
state dashboard, cutoffs (shift) 11
student achievement: beliefs 22; impact 11, 48
student growth mindset: development 31; focus 32–33
student health/wellness departments, formative data usage 22
student information system (SIS): access 57–58; data syncing requirements 64; formative data reports 66; formative data system, building 51–52; real-time data 64–65; syncing 66; updated information, usage 64; vendor, contact 64
student learning: achievement, knowledge 84–85; beliefs/role, reflection 21–24; capability, development (self-assessment) 34; commitment 37; content, selection

85; difficulty 84, 85; experiences, responses 85; support 55; vision 19
students: day-to-day experiences 53; education 34; evidence, analysis 32; experience (transformation), growth mindset (approach) 33, 35; needs 8; physical/mental well-being, influence 22; services departments, real-time formative data usage 22; strengths, building 111; subgroups, risk/support 71; support (impact), real-time formative data (usage) 7; time/support, identification 85; work, revision opportunity 31
student success: ensuring 18, 22, 117; formative data, impact 31; impact 6, 12, 93; increase 20; role 36
success: celebration events, best practice sharing (usage) 115–118; culture, creation 35; increase 20; stories, sharing 86
summative data: gathering 55; importance 106; loss 10–11; outcomes 109; principals, attention 34; prioritization 109; public availability 109; real-time formative data, comparison 105–106
summative data points: availability 112; limitations 10–11
summative state data 70
symbolic data use/misuse/abuse 52
systematic plan, student requirements 85

teachers: change, openness 113; differentiated PD opportunities 21; practices, systematic inquiry 7; real-time formative data usage 22; role, beliefs (reflection) 21–24; vision, establishment 19
technological tools, usage 53
technology: advancements 12; incorporation 53; influx 5; reference 27; support 7; usage 6, 99
templates, usage 52
topic areas, listing 58
training sessions, strategies 88
transparency, function 71–72

validation concerns, identification/addressing 70–72
videoconferencing 86; technology, usage 88
virtual peer observations 87–91
vision 123; core 39; factors 22; impact 82; language, inclusion 20; organizational vision, requirement 84; progress, assessment (timing) 25; real-time formative data, inclusion 20; reevaluation 18; reflection 19; sharing 25; shift, impact 18
visual presentations, usage 39
visual techniques, usage 24

For Product Safety Concerns and Information please contact our EU
representative GPSR@taylorandfrancis.com
Taylor & Francis Verlag GmbH, Kaufingerstraße 24, 80331 München, Germany

www.ingramcontent.com/pod-product-compliance
Lightning Source LLC
Chambersburg PA
CBHW061451300426
44114CB00014B/1933